RAGHU PALAT is an acknowledged authority on investment, finance and banking and has written more than thirty extremely well received books on these subjects.

A great grandson of His Highness, the late Rama Varma, Maharaja of Cochin and Sir Chettur Sankaran Nair (a member of the Viceroy's Privy Council and a former President of the Indian National Congress), Raghu Palat is a Fellow of the Institute of Chartered Accountants in England & Wales.

A career banker he has held very senior positions with multinational banks in India and abroad. He has worked in Europe, America, Asia and Africa.

Raghu Palat is presently a consultant to banks. He also manages a dedicated finance portal called www.bankingrules.com which is a repertoire of rules and regulations relating to finance, commerce, corporates and banks. In addition, he conducts workshops on business etiquette, effective business writing, presentation skills, banking and finance.

Mr. Palat has also set up a portal for e-learning www.ibbc.co.in. The courses are an amalgam of laws, directives and actual real life situations.

Raghu Palat lives in Mumbai with his wife Pushpa, two daughters, Divya and Nikhila and their cocker spaniel Champ.

"This book brims with accurate, immediate and relevant examples of Indian companies and our stock market behaviour" *Indian Review of Books*

"Educates readers" *The Economic Times*

Also by Raghu Palat

Fiction

Anguish

Non Fiction

Tax Planning for the Salaried Employee

The Credit Report

The Magic of Ratios

The Wonderworld of Investments

Understanding Ratios

How to Read Annual Reports and Balance Sheets

Investments — Where and When

Understanding Financial Ratios in Business

Shares for Investment and Wealth

Documentary Letters of Credit and Collections

How to Apply for a Bank Loan and Get it Sanctioned

How to Manage Foreign Exchange Risks

Effective Business Writing

A Complete Guide for the NRI

Everything Indians Need to Know on Business Etiquette

Interview Tips — Get the Job You Want

Secrets of their Success — Achievers from the World of Finance

Corporate Leaders — Secrets of their Success

Self Made High Achievers — Secrets of their Success

The Bank of India Story — Relationships Beyond Banking

The Negotiable Instruments Act

Retail Banking

Marketing of Banking Services

Banking Fundamentals

Basic Banking

Basics of Banking

Advances and Credit Analysis

The Write Way to Success

Corporate Banking — Everything You Need to Know to Work in a Bank

Mutual Funds — Everything You Need to Know

FUNDAMENTAL ANALYSIS FOR INVESTORS

HOW TO MAKE CONSISTENT, LONG-TERM PROFITS IN THE STOCK MARKET

RAGHU PALAT

www.visionbooksindia.com

To my mother-in-law
Vasanta A. Nair

www.visionbooksindia.com

Disclaimer

The author and the publisher disclaim all legal or other responsibilities for any losses which investors may suffer by investing or trading using the methods described in this book. Readers are advised to seek professional guidance before making any specific investments. This book is meant purely for the purpose of investor and trader education.

First Published 1994, Second Edition, 2000, Third Edition, 2004, Fourth Edition, 2010, 15th Reprint, 2024

ISBN 10: 81-7094-795-2
ISBN 13: 978-81-7094-795-0

Published by
Vision Books Pvt. Ltd.
(Incorporating Orient Paperbacks and CARING Imprints)
24 Feroze Gandhi Road, Lajpat Nagar 3
New Delhi 110024, India.
Phone: (+91-11) 2984 0821 / 22
e-mail: visionbooks@gmail.com

Printed at
Ashim Print Line
38/2, 35 &36 Sahibabad Industrial Area, Ghaziabad
Uttar Pradesh 201010, India.

Contents

Part Three

Company Analysis

Preface

The Indian capital market is vibrant and alive. Its growth in the last three decades has been phenomenal. In 1983, market capitalization of the shares quoted in the Bombay Stock Exchange amounted to a mere US $7 billion. It grew to US $65 billion in 1992; to US $220 billion by April 2000; to US $ 428 billion in 2003, and hit US $ 1,350 billion (Indian Rs. 60,78,034 crore) in May 2010. Not just that. In May 2010, 4,078 companies were quoted on the Bombay Stock Exchange making it one of the largest such exchange in the world.

The ride has been tumultuous. The growth of the market began with the FERA dilution, i.e. when foreign companies were compelled to dilute their holdings in their Indian entities. The interest in the stock market grew with speculators and others entering the arena. Though one may question their methods, individuals such as the late Harshad Mehta must be recognized as people who did much to create an awareness of the market which led India's middle class to start investing in shares. The reforms following the liberalization of the early 1990s, the entry into this market of foreign institutional investors (FIIs) and mutual funds, coupled with scams and downturns, forced many an individual investor out of the market. The bursting of the dotcom bubble and the Ketan Parekh scam heightened the average investor's fears. It is interesting to note that the individual who invested in the market during the boom in the third quarter of 2003 is the young, new generation investor — investors who had not lost monies in the earlier Harshad Mehta or Ketan Parekh scams. Then in the boom of 2006-07, the index soared culminating at 21,078 on 8 January 2008 before falling to below 10,000 within a year in the wake of the world wide economic depression.

And, yet, the investor dreams even after he has been mauled. This is because the share market can make one wealthy beyond one's wildest dreams. With the boom in IT shares, for example, Azim Premji of Wipro was for a brief period the second richest man in the world (after buffetting away Warren Buffett from that position) and Infosys Chairman K Narayanamurthy was, at one time, worth in excess of Rs. 14,000 crore.

During the last two decades, the manner of trading in the markets has changed — from the traditional floor (trading ring) outcry to screen based trading with brokers linked to the major stock exchanges. Shares that are traded in stock exchanges are now dematerialized — making sales / purchases and transfers easy. Payment for shares sold is made within a few days.

Information has exploded. At one time there was an acute dearth. Now it is like a tornado. There are very good reports on companies. There are probing analyses done on performance. There are studied forecasts made. There are intelligent conclusions drawn. The information is there. Any investor can access it. And the investor must access it and having accessed it, he must, manage the information.

In terms of categories of investors, the largest investor segment in the Indian stock market is that of the financial institutions and mutual funds. Foreign institutional investors (FIIs) and Non-Resident Indians (NRIs), too, have a significant presence.

By mid-2010, they accounted for about 12% of the investments made in the market. FIIs often impact market movement far beyond their actual share because they can and do move large amounts of money in and out of the market owing to their global perspective.

Notwithstanding the considerable institutionalisation of the Indian market is, it is still rumour and insider driven. Even after the many scams, shares continue to be bought on the basis of tips, and for the short term. The average investor does little or no research (even though more information than he can handle is now available) and makes his purchase or sale decision on the strength of an article that he may have read or a conversation with a friend. This is usually because the average investor is unclear on how to analyze companies and is not equipped to arrive at an investment decision. Consequently, he buys and sells with inadequate information and often suffers needless losses. At no time was this more evident than in the first four months of 1992 and later in 2000 when even prices of the "dogs" doubled. It was a period not dissimilar to Wall Street in the mid 1960s which Mr. Harold Q. Masur eloquently described in his book, *The Broker*:

> "In the super heated economy of the late sixties there was an illusion of endless prosperity. On Wall Street the bulls were rampant. Private companies were going public at arbitrary prices that generated huge profits for the promoters. Mutual funds were plunging recklessly into new untested issues. Glamour stocks soared to premiums that discounted not only the future but the next millennium. Money, it seemed, was spermatic. Properly invested in the womb of Wall Street, it would produce wildly proliferating offspring. Thousands of new comers opened accounts. Brokerage firms expanded with quixotic optimism."

As I write this (May 2010), the market is buoyant after two years of being in the doldrums. Experts are prophesying with gay abandon, "The market will grow to 20,000 by Diwali." Another says, "The market (Sensex) will rise to 30,000 by June 2012." These are numbers taken out of a hat. They have no logic. They have no credibility. Yet, there are so many gullible investors who, fuelled by greed, buy high and then live to regret having done so. Human nature has not changed.

I'd like you to dwell for a moment on a thought by Harold Masur. He says:

> "Bargains are available during times of extreme pessimism. Trouble is, when the so-called experts are wringing their hands, nobody has the courage to buy".

Rothschild echoed this when he said, "Buy when there is blood on the streets."

J. P. Morgan when asked once by an investor on his view of the market is said to have stated: "It will fluctuate." Some will rise while others will fall. The aim of the investor must be to buy when the price is low and to sell when it is high.

Fundamental analysis is not for speculators. It is for those who are prepared to study and analyze a company; for those who arrive at a decision after careful thought and deliberation. Hegel once said, "To those who look upon the world rationally, the world in its turn presents a rational aspect." Fundamental analysis is for the rational man.

This book is for the investor — be he or she an executive, a housewife, a professional, a student or a self-employed person. My aim is to introduce you to the world of information and analysis and to show you how one can arrive at a buy or sell decision. By doing so, I seek to discourage you from acting on rumours or tips and encourage you to go by hard facts.

However, the investor must be warned that the world is constantly changing as a consequence of which new situations arise which the investor must continuously monitor. Consequently, there is no fixed formula that will give one "wealth beyond belief". If such a formula existed, I wouldn't be writing this book. I would be out there in the market accumulating that wealth. Analysis and information give one the basis for a logical decision. There are other factors, especially the human factor, that are sometimes not logical and cannot be predicted.

To select the most promising shares, the investor faces obstacles. The first is in the assessment — the human fallibility factor. The second arises from the nature of competition. The third is from sheer perversity — the failure of the market to be logical. The investor may be wrong in his estimate of the future or even if he is right the current price may already reflect what he is anticipating. The point I am trying to stress is that in the end, the price movements of shares depend on a host of factors. Yet the basic issue remains. The share must have value. Its fundamentals must be good. Its management must be competent. This book will introduce you to the world of fundamental analysis and guide you through the factors that you should look at before you buy any shares.

The art of successful investment lies in the choice of those industries that are most likely to grow in the future and then in identifying the most promising companies in those industries. There are, however, pitfalls in the approach and one must be careful. It must, however, be remembered that:

- Obvious prospects for physical growth in a business do not translate into obvious profits for investors.
- Experts do not have dependable ways of concentrating on the most promising companies in the most promising industries.

There could also be imbalances on account of political happenings, speculations, demand and a host of other reasons. Further, as Adam Smith said:

> "Even if, by some magic, you knew the future growth rate of the little darling you just discovered, you do not really know how the market will capitalize that growth. Sometimes the market will pay twenty times earnings for company growing at an annual compounded rate of 30 percent; sometimes it will pay sixty times earnings for the same company. Sometime the market goes on a growth binge, especially when bonds and the more traditional securities do not seem to offer intriguing alternatives. At other times the alternatives are enticing enough to draw away some of the money that goes into pursuing growth. It all depends in the psychological climate of the time."

That is why he also added:

> "You can have no preconceived ideas. There are fundamentals in the market place, but the unexplored area is the emotional area. All the charts and breadth indicators and technical players are the statisticians attempts to describe an emotional state."

This is why finance theory does not support the belief that the fundamental approach, or for that matter any other approach be it technical analysis, random walk, etc. can consistently outperform the market. However, fundamental analysis gives you a fighting chance and it is because of this that I urge you to be familiar with it and practise it when you go out to do battle.

I'd like to leave you with an observation made by the then Finance Minister, Mr. Yashwant Sinha on 4 May 2000 after offering certain tax sops at the budget session. He said:

"I can appreciate a market responding to fundamentals, but a market which responds to rumours is irresponsible and silly. The BSE (Bombay Stock Exchange) is being driven by rumours, they will have to behave more responsibly."

Benjamin Graham adds:

"The investor's chief problem is likely to be himself. More money has been made and kept by ordinary people who were temperamentally well suited for the investment process than by those who lacked this quality even though they had extensive knowledge of finance, accounting and stock market lore."

In summary, the purpose of this book is to help you invest in stocks that have value; that have good fundamentals. Santayana once said: "Those who do not remember the past are condemned to return to it." Benjamin Graham added to this by saying, "To invest intelligently in securities one should be forearmed with an adequate knowledge of how the various types of stocks have behaved under varying conditions – some of which one is likely to meet again in one's experience." This book attempts to arm you.

May 2010 RAGHU PALAT

Acknowledgements

I met Kapil Malhotra of Vision Books in the first quarter of 1993. He met me unannounced and at a time when I was in the midst of a dilemma — the dilemma of whether I should write another book on accounting and pure finance. It was he who suggested, after listening very patiently, that I should consider, not a book on pure finance but on fundamental analysis. I confess that this was a thought I had not considered and the more I thought of it, the more it made sense. I must therefore thank Kapil for the idea and constant encouragement and it is because of him that this book has been written.

Nobody, other than a professional writer, can have the time to devote to writing after a full working day, unless practically all his responsibilities are borne by another. My wife Pushpa is wonderful. She works as I do and she has practically single-handedly brought up both our children, Divya and Nikhila, beautifully. She sits with them in the evenings, helping them with their homework thereby giving me the time and space to write. Without her love, support and encouragement, I would not have been able to write a single line — let alone numerous books. I am indeed fortunate in having such a wife.

I must thank the other members of my family too — my daughters Divya and Nikhila, my brother Ravi, my father-in-law,

K. V. A. Nair, and my mother-in-law, Vasanta Nair. One of my father-in-law's greatest dreams — and the greatest challenge of his life — has been to interest my mother-in-law in the fascinating world of shares. Alas and alack he struggles on — the end is not in sight as yet. I dedicate this book to that charming lady, my mother-in-law Vasanta Nair in the hope that she will read this book from cover to cover and become fascinated by shares. Thus, my father-in-law's dream will be realised.

Introduction

The Importance of Information

"The market," says Mr. Johnson in Adam Smith's *The Money Game*, "is like a beautiful woman — endlessly fascinating, endlessly complex, always changing, always mystifying. I have been absorbed and immersed since 1924 and I know this is no science. It is an art. Now we have computers and all sorts of statistics but the market is still the same and understanding the market is still no easier. It is personal intuition, sensing patterns of behaviour. There is always something unknown, undiscerned." The market is fascinating and addictive and once you have entered it "it is foolish to think that you can withdraw from the exchange after you have tasted the sweetness of the honey", De La Vega commented in the seventeenth century.

The lure of the market is the promise of great wealth. Warren Buffett has been for several years one of the wealthiest men in the world. His net worth was estimated by *Forbes* in 2010 to be $ 47 billion. The wealth is entirely from the market — by managing an investing company called Hathaway. He believes in value investing — in fundamental analysis. It is the promise of great wealth, of emulating persons like Buffett and his gurus Benjamin Graham and Bernard Baruch that spurs investors on. This lure was demonstrated in India in 1992, at the end of the millennium (in the first 4 months of 2000), from the end of the second quarter of 2003, and more recently in 2006 and 2007 when prices soared. The manner in which these speculative drives occur are similar and happens with amazing frequency and regularity. This is not restricted to shares either. The tulip mania in Holland in the seventeenth century sent their prices soaring. In 1992, the rush to buy shares in India was so great that ancestral land and family jewels were sold or pawned in the overpowering, overwhelming greed for riches. For a time, prices rose and then the bubble burst. This occurred again in early 2000 when information technology share prices rose to phenomenal heights. Many shrewd promoters changed the names of their companies to "infotech", or added the word "infotech" to its name and made a killing in the market. The law of gravity has to prevail and their prices fell dramatically in March and April 2000, supporting the truth that prices of companies will fall or rise to their true level in time. The prices of shares rose as the crowd had taken over and there was no place then for logic or good sense. As Gustave Le Bon observed in his *Psychologic des Toules*, the crowd acts with a single-minded purpose and not very rationally. According to him, the most striking peculiarity of a crowd is that "whoever be the individuals that compose it, however like or unlike be their mode of life, their occupations, their character of their intelligence, the fact that they have been transformed into a crowd puts them in possession of a sort of collective mind which makes them feel, think, and act in a manner different from that in which each individual of them would feel, think, and act were he in a state of isolation". Le Bon speaks of the crowd being in a state of hypnotized fascination and the rational investor becoming mindless in the sense that he surrenders his rational thinking mind to the dominant mood of the moment. The crowd in late 1999 and early 2000 everywhere, and in India in 1992 and again in 2006 and 2007, acted on impulse, on expectations and hope and on hearsay fuelled by greed. The index bloated like a balloon and like a balloon it burst. It had to. Unfortunately at times such as these the ones that lose are the small investors who do not have their eye on the market at all times, nor do they have the contacts or wherewithal to know what is likely to happen to the market.

Let us examine what happened in the last two decades in India. In 1992, investors were buying on the flimsiest of reasons believing there was no end to the boom. I remember a person advising me to buy the shares of a certain company. This was at the time not a very well known company. I asked him for some information — what did the company do? Who were its directors? How had it performed in the last three years? He did not know, nor did he care. He had received a tip that the price would double and was passing it on. Another share that must be mentioned was Karnataka Ball Bearings — a company whose share was languishing in the low 20s. Sparked by a rumour that Harshad Mehta was buying the share, its price rose to Rs. 60, then to Rs. 68 and went all the way up to Rs. 180, all in matter of just ten days. It was then heard that the rumour about Harshad Mehta's interest in the share was false. The share price plunged to Rs. 50 in four days. The original rumour raised its head. The price rose again to Rs. 120. The rumour was again condemned as false and the price fell. At that time I spoke with a person intimately connected with the company. He told me that the company was sick and that there was no business activity. In fact, it was on the verge of closing down. The price had risen on the flimsiest of excuses and the crowd comprising of otherwise intelligent, logical and rational human beings, acted irrationally and illogically. A lot of persons did make money on the stock — but most lost, having bought it with no other information than the rumour that Harshad Mehta was buying the share. One would have thought one learns. Not so.

History repeats itself. At the end of the last century Indian shares, especially those related to Information Technology (IT), such as Wipro, Infosys (lovingly called Infy) and Satyam (Sify) began to be quoted in America in the NASDAQ. With the rise in NASDAQ, these shares began rising and a wave feeling took over that software was the new mantra and that the shares of all IT companies could only go one way — up. Thus began an upward movement that gained momentum every day till prices became unreal. The wise began to exit and as this took root prices began to fall. This had a snowballing effect and soon prices had fallen by more than 50%. Then, later, when the dotcom boom occurred, shares were priced on the basis of "stickiness of eyeballs". It is impossible to get more esoteric. Later in 2000 people began buying shares that Ketan Parekh was purportedly buying. The question that begs an answer is, "Will investors never learn?" The answer probably is that man's greed is bottomless.

In 2003, prices again began moving upwards. The Sensex broke through the 5,000 barrier and there were many who predicted that it would reach 6,000 in six months/ one year/ very soon. In 2006 and 2007 there was an unprecedented surge in the Sensex. It culminated on 8 January 2008 when the Sensex closed at 21,078. At that time it was predicted the Sensex would cross 50,000 within a few months. Many buy on the "strength" of these predictions which are nothing but predictions, hopes, expectations. Nothing backed by logic or sense.

Fundamental analysis submits that no one should purchase a share on a whim. Investment in shares is serious business and all aspects and factors, however minor, must be analyzed and considered. The billionaire Jean Paul Getty, until his death the richest man in the world, once said, "No one should buy (a share) without knowing as much as possible about the company that issues it". Jim Slater was one of the most successful stock pickers of all time. He evolved a theory called the Zulu theory which submits that one must know all about the company and the industry, and any other factor that may affect the company's performance. His argument was that one could never lose if one has this information. If the company is likely to do badly, one can sell and then buy shares to cover this when the price falls, and *vice versa.* This is the philosophy of professional and successful investors — informed investing. And this is the foremost tenet of fundamental analysis. As Adam Smith says, "There is no substitute for information. The market is not a roulette wheel. Good research and good ideas are the one absolute necessity in the market place."

Fundamental analysis demands, nay insists, on solid information about a company. It requires subjecting a company's performance and its financial statements to the most piercing scrutiny as well as the analysis of the economy and the industry in which the company operates. The fundamentalist then makes his buy or sell decision on the basis of his interpretation of the information that he receives, his analysis, and on the strength of his experience and investment maturity.

All information is important and can be grouped under the following classifications:

1. Information about the economy.
2. Information about government policy; taxation, levies, duties and others.

3. Information about the industry in which the company operates.
4. Information about the company — its management, its performance, its sales and its products including its performance in relation to other similar companies.
5. Information about consumer outlook, fashions and spending.

In India, we are fortunate that there is greater awareness of the need for information today than ever before and this need is being addressed by the media, researchers and professional investment consultants.

Internet

The internet is a tremendous source of information. It can tell you about the economy, company results, profiles and a host of other information. Now can even buy and sell shares instantly on the Net.

Media

There are several investment and business focused magazines, newspapers and directories available today that discuss the economy, industries and individual companies. These contain articles of a high standard that analyze industries and companies in depth. They also contain knowledgeable articles on tax, investment strategies, finance and allied subjects.

I would insist that the serious investor should read at least one good financial paper every day and two magazines a month. This ought to keep him well informed.

Investment Newsletters

There are several professional investment managers and experts who publish investment information. This is extremely useful as they are often very up-to-date and contain information not generally available to the investor.

Insiders

Insiders are persons who work for a company or who have intimate dealings with a company and have access to, or are aware of, information that is not generally known. This could be information on the performance of the company, upcoming rights or bonus issues, or some other relevant news. As the information is not known to all, the investor must act fast if he wishes to make a killing. The Securities Exchange Board of India (SEBI) has published regulations prohibiting insider trading. I would also caution against insider trading; apart from the fact that it is against SEBI rules and the law, it is fraught with other risks. Edwin Leferre, in his book, *Reminiscences of a Stockbroker* also warned against it saying, "Wall Street professionals know that acting on inside tips will break a man more quickly than famine, pestilence, crop failure, political readjustments or what may be called normal accidents."

Seminars and Lectures by Investment Experts

Excellent seminars and lectures are being held in the country. These are conducted by eminent individuals and one can pick up a lot of information by attending these lectures. These may be on how an industry is doing, their view of an industry, and the like. One can even share thoughts with those they meet. This can result in forming opinions. Acting on these opinions could be profitable.

Stockbrokers

Stockbrokers are always in touch with companies and are normally aware of their performance and other factors affecting the price of a share. However, it should be remembered that:

- Stockbrokers usually view companies from a short term point of view.
- A lot of information that a broker gives is based on rumours and tips — many of which may be untrue and unsubstantiated.
- Stockbrokers sometimes describe companies glowingly based on hearsay; this could be misleading.
- Brokers may also give you information to make you buy the shares they want to offload.

These are the major sources of information. You must train yourself to listen and absorb information that you receive. You should analyze and interpret the information to determine the profitable course of action to be taken. This is the essential governing principle of fundamental analysis — action only after receiving and analyzing information.

It is also extremely important that one acts swiftly on the information received as the person who receives it first will often be the person to profit most from it. That is what Rothschild did.

18 June 1815, was a date that will be remembered as the day when one of the most decisive battles in Europe was fought — the day the Duke of Wellington pitted his 75,000 English troops against the 100,000 soldiers of Napoleon. The battle was mo-

mentous as the future of Europe and the European colonies around the world rested on its outcome.

Investors in London were concerned and worried. As the German army under Marshal Von Blucher had not joined its English ally at the time the battle began, there was concern that England would lose the battle. The British East India Company's trade with India and China was threatened. There was fear that its allies might desert England. The future of the English Empire was at stake.

Investors awaited news. Nathan Rothschild of the House of Rothschild, a leading merchant banker, aware of the importance of information, had invested a considerable sum to develop a private intelligence system. This was well known. It was also well known that Rothschild had invested heavily on an English victory. As soon as the war was over, Rothschild's agents dispatched to him carrier pigeons with the result of the war in code. When they arrived, well before the official dispatches, Rothschild began to sell every thing he owned. In the belief that the English had lost, investors panicked and began to sell. The market collapsed. In the depressed market, Rothschild stepped in and, along with his agents bought and bought. Within hours, the news of Wellington's victory sent the market booming. By this manoeuvre, Rothschild earned one million pounds, a fabulous amount at that time and it is this that led him to state, "The best time to buy is when blood is running in the streets".

Chapter One

Fundamental Analysis

The Search for Intrinsic Value

Fundamental analysis is based on the premise that every share has a certain intrinsic value at a period of time. This intrinsic value changes from time to time as a consequence of both internal and external factors. The theory of fundamental analysis submits that one should purchase a share when it is available below its intrinsic value and sell it when it rises above its intrinsic value. When the market value of a share is below its intrinsic value it is under valued, whereas if the market value of a share is above its intrinsic value it is over valued. Fundamentalists thus seek to purchase underpriced shares and sell overpriced ones. They believe that although the market price may deviate from the intrinsic value in the short term, in the long term the market price will be equal to the intrinsic value.

What is Intrinsic Value

What is the intrinsic value of a share? How is it determined? Fundamental analysis propounds that the intrinsic value is, and has to be, based on the benefits that accrue to investors in the share. As the return to shareholders is in the form of dividends, under strict fundamental analysis, the present value of future dividends discounted on the basis of its perceived safety or risk is its intrinsic value. The intrinsic value is based on the dividend because that is what a shareholder or investor receives from a company, and not on the earnings per share of the company. This distinction is very important.

Calculation of Intrinsic Value

How, then, does one calculate the intrinsic value of a share? Let us assume that one expects a return of 20% on an investment every year for 3 years. Let us also assume that the company would pay dividends of 20%, 25% and 30% on its Rs. 10 share. The dividend received on a share would therefore be Rs. 2.00 in the first year, Rs. 2.50 in the second, and Rs. 3.00 in the third. Let us also assume that the share can be sold at Rs. 200 at the end of 3 years.

The intrinsic value of the share will be:

$$\frac{2}{1.2}+\frac{2.5}{(1.2)^2}+\frac{3+200}{(1.2)^3}=\text{Rs.}120.88$$

The logic is to discount the dividend received and anticipated to be received in future years and the expected price at a future date with the return or yield expected. Since the price at that future date is also considered, the possibility of capital appreciation is considered and this is why this method of arriving at the intrinsic value is considered the most balanced and fair.

If the market price of the share is below Rs. 120.88 then the share is below its intrinsic value and therefore well worth purchasing. If, on the other hand, the market price is higher, it is a sell signal and the share should be sold.

Considerations

It must be noted that the intrinsic value of a share can and will be different for different individuals. If, in regard to the above mentioned investment another individual (Kumar) expects a return of 16% whereas a third individual (Nair) expects a return of 25%, the intrinsic value (assuming the dividends and the sale value at the end of 3 years will remain the same will be) —

Intrinsic value for Kumar:

$$\frac{2}{1.16} + \frac{2.5}{(1.16)^2} + \frac{3 + 200}{(1.16)^3} = \text{Rs.}133.63$$

Intrinsic value for Nair:

$$\frac{2}{1.25} + \frac{2.5}{(1.25)^2} + \frac{3 + 200}{(1.25)^3} = \text{Rs.}107.14$$

Thus if the market price is Rs. 120.88, the first individual (let us call him Siddharth) will hold onto the share whereas Nair would sell the share and Kumar would purchase it. In short, the intrinsic value of a share will vary from individual to individual and will be dependant both on that individual's ability to bear risks and the return that individual expects.

It is prudent and logical to remove this anomaly. The return expected should be the return one can expect from an alternate, reasonably safe investment in that market. This rate should be bolstered by a risk factor as the return is greater from riskier investments. A very safe investment (blue chip) will have a risk rate of 0. A mature near blue chip share will have a risk rate of 1. A growing company will have a risk rate of 2. A risky new company will have a risk rate of 3. If it is assumed that the return one can expect from a reasonably safe investment (an investment say with the Unit Trust of India) is 16%, and the dividend expected is Rs. 2 in the first year, Rs. 2.5 in the second year and Rs. 3 in the third year and the anticipated sale price is expected to be Rs. 200, the intrinsic value of the share of the company will be as follows depending on its financial strength and stage of growth:

Blue Chip $$\frac{2}{1.16}+\frac{2.5}{(1.16)^2}+\frac{3+200}{(1.16)^3}=\text{Rs.}133.63$$

Mature Share $$\frac{2}{1.17}+\frac{2.5}{(1.17)^2}+\frac{3+200}{(1.17)^3}=\text{Rs.}130.28$$

Growing Company $$\frac{2}{1.18}+\frac{2.5}{(1.18)^2}+\frac{3+200}{(1.18)^3}=\text{Rs.}127.04$$

New Company $$\frac{2}{1.19}+\frac{2.5}{(1.19)^2}+\frac{3+200}{(1.19)^3}=\text{Rs.}123.91$$

It would be noted that the safer the share, the higher its intrinsic value.

There is however one factor that is assumed or estimated and that is the price at the end of three years. The most reasonable method (even though this is arguable), in my opinion is basing the price on a price earnings multiple. The price earnings multiple or P/E of a share is its market price divided by its earnings per share. If a company has earned Rs. 7 per share in the current year representing a growth of 20% and if it is conservatively believed that the earnings per share (EPS) will grow 15% every year:

- EPS at the end of: Year 1 will be Rs. 7.70
- EPS at the end of: Year 2 will be Rs. 8.47
- EPS at the end of: Year 3 will be Rs. 9.32.

If it is believed that a reasonable P/E for a company of such a size in that industry should be 15, the market price at the end of 3 years would be 9.32 × 15 = Rs. 139.80.

Let us now look at a real example. On 31 May 2010 the price of the shares of a company was Rs. 465 The company declared a dividend of 65% for the year ended 31 March 2010 and an earnings per share of Rs. 13.3. If we assume that this dividend will remain constant, and that a P/E of 20 is reasonable, the intrinsic value of the company's share should be Rs. 266. If the company's earnings grow at 20% per year the EPS at the end of 3 years would be Rs. 22.98 (13.3 x 1.20 x 1.20 x 1.20). On that assumption, the price at the end of 3 years would be Rs. 459.60 (EPS × P/E of 20). Based on an expected return of 20%, the intrinsic value today will therefore be:

$$\frac{6.5}{1.20}+\frac{6.5}{(1.20)^2}+\frac{6.5+459.60}{(1.20)^3} = \text{Rs. } 279.66$$

The company's share price at Rs. 465 was thus nearly 67% above its intrinsic value and on the basis of this submission should be sold.

The price of a 100% export oriented unit on 31 May 2010 was 160. Its profit in the year to 31 March 2010 had grown by 60% to Rs. 17.88 crore. Its earnings per share at Rs. 10.26 was an improvement of 23%. If we assume that in the next 2 years its EPs will grow by 20%, the EPS at the end of 2 years would be Rs. 14.77. At a P/E of 15, its market price at the end of 2 years would be Rs. 221.55. In 2010, the company paid a dividend of 25%. On the assumption that the dividend of 25% will be maintained in 2011, and that it will rise to 30% in 2005, its intrinsic value on an expected return of 20% would be:

$$\frac{2.5}{1.2}+\frac{3.0+221.55}{(1.2)^2} = \text{Rs.} 158.02$$

Its intrinsic value of Rs. 158.02 was very close to the market value of Rs. 160.

If however, one expects a return of 25% as that export oriented unit is a relatively new company, the intrinsic value would be:

$$\frac{2.5}{1.25}+\frac{3.0+221.55}{(1.2)^2}=\text{Rs.}145.71$$

At an expected return of 25%, the market value of Rs. 160 was higher than the intrinsic value of Rs. 145.71 and the share should be sold.

The subjective assumptions made in arriving at the intrinsic value results in the intrinsic value of a share being different for different individuals. In the example detailed above, the intrinsic value of that company share would be Rs. 158.02 for an investor who expects a return of 20%, whereas it would be Rs. 145.71 for an individual expecting a return of 25%. The other assumptions too are subjective, i.e. the expected price at the end of a period, and the anticipated dividends during the period.

This method, however, is extremely logical. It considers the dividends that will be paid and the likely capital appreciation that will take place.

Efficient Market Theory

Fundamental analysts often use the efficient market theory in determining the intrinsic price of a share. This theory submits that in an efficient market all investors receive information instantly and that it is understood and analyzed by all the market players and is immediately reflected in the market prices. The market price, therefore, at every point in time represents the latest position at all times. The efficient market theory submits it is not possible to make profits looking at old data or by studying the patterns of previous price changes. It assumes that all foreseeable events have already been built into the current market price. Thus, to work out the likely future price at a future date in order to determine the share's present intrinsic value, fundamentalists devote time and effort to ascertain the effect of various happenings (present and future) on the profitability of the company and its likely results. This must also include the possibility of the company issuing bonus shares or offering rights shares.

The most important factor in fundamental analysis is information — information about the economy, the industry and the company itself — any information that can affect the growth and profitability of the company and it is because of this fundamental analysis is broken into three distinct parts:

1. The economy,
2. The industry within which the company operates, and
3. The company.

The information has to be interpreted and analyzed and the intrinsic value of the share determined. This intrinsic value must, then, be compared against the market value the fundamentalists say, and only then can an investment decision be taken.

Part One

Economic Analysis

Chapter Two

Politico-Economic Analysis

A wise man once said, "No man is an island." No person can work and live in isolation. External forces are constantly influencing an individual's actions and affecting him. Similarly, no industry or company can exist in isolation. It may have splendid managers and a tremendous product. However, its sales and its costs are affected by factors, some of which are beyond its control — the world economy, price inflation, taxes and a host of others. It is important, therefore, to have an appreciation of the politico-economic factors that affect an industry and a company.

The Political Equation

A stable political environment is necessary for steady, balanced growth. If a country is ruled by a stable government which takes decisions for the long-term development of the country, industry and companies will prosper. On the other hand, instability causes insecurity, especially if there is the possibility of a government being ousted and replaced by another that holds diametrically different political and economic beliefs.

India has gone through a fairly difficult period. There had been terrible political instability after the ouster of Mr.

Narasimha Rao from the Prime Ministership. Successive elections held did not give any single political party a clear majority and mandate. As a result there were coalitions of unlikes. These led to considerable jockeying for power and led to the breakup of the governments and fresh elections. There has also been much grand standing such as the Mandal recommendations in order to capture votes. These led to riots. There were other religious and ethnic issues that also led to violence such as the Babri Masjid/Ram Janmabhoomi issue. There were Hindu-Muslim disturbances and bomb blasts. All these shook the confidence of the developed world in the security and stability of India. Tourism fell. Foreign Direct Investment fell. Investments were held back. These had an adverse impact on the development of the economy. In recent times this scenario has changed. The Government, even though a coalition one has been stable. Its policies have been positive and the economy has been doing well. There are predictions that by 2050, India would be one of the three most powerful nations in the world. This has led to renewed interest in India and investors are back.

International events too impact industries and companies. The USSR was one of India's biggest purchasers. When that enormous country broke up into the Confederation of Independent States, Indian exports declined and this affected the profitability of companies who had to search for other markets. Wars have a similar effect. The war in Croatia, in Kosovo, in Africa, the Gulf war and other wars have had an effect on exports of goods. The tragedy of 9/11 (September 9 when two planes crashed into the World Trade Center at New York), affected the entire world. Many industries are yet to fully recover. Similarly the SARS epidemic that affected South East Asia affected trade and tourism.

The other gnawing political issue that is a thorn in India's back is the Pakistan issue. The deterioration in our relationship culminated in 1999 in the war in Kargil. Earlier we have fought several wars on Kashmir and other issues. Wars push up inflation and demand declines. It is estimated that the Gulf War cost India $1.5 billion on account of higher prices of petroleum products, opportunity costs and fall in exports. The defence budget is enormous. This money could have been spent elsewhere for the development of the country. Other examples include Sri Lanka, East Europe and other troubled countries. These countries were once thriving. No longer. Let us take the example of Sri Lanka. It is a beautiful island and was considered a paradise for tourists — a pearl in the ocean. The country is in the grips of a civil war. The northern part of the country, which was once thriving, is in the hands of Tamil guerillas and there is no industry and little economic activity. Idi Amin in the seventies by expelling Asians from Uganda did that country's economy irreparable harm. In 1997-98, due to the elections and then the bombing of the American embassy, the economy of Kenya tailspinned to negative growth. Then a few years later as the economy was recovering, the Mombasa bombings again set it back.

In conclusion, the political stability of a country is of paramount importance. No industry or company can grow and prosper in the midst of political turmoil.

Foreign Exchange Reserves

A country needs foreign exchange reserves to meet its commitments, pay for its imports and service foreign debts. Without foreign exchange, a country would not be able to import materials or goods for its development and there is also a loss of international confidence in such a country. In 1991, India was national confidence in such a country. In 1991, India was forced to devalue the rupee as our foreign exchange reserves were, at $532 million very low, barely enough for few weeks' imports. The crisis was averted at that time by an IMF loan, the pledging of gold, and the devaluation of the rupee.

Several North American banks had to write off large loans advanced to South American countries when these countries were unable to make repayments. Certain African countries too have very low foreign exchange reserves. Companies exporting to such countries have to be careful as the importing companies may not be able to pay for their purchases because the country does not have adequate foreign exchange. I know of an Indian company which had exported machines to an African company a few years ago. The importing company paid the money to its bank. It lies there still. The payment could not be sent to India as the central bank refused the foreign exchange to make the payment. Following the liberalization moves initiated by the Narasimha Rao Government and endorsed/supported by successive governments, India had by 31 December 1999 foreign investments in excess of $28 billion. In May 2000, the foreign exchange reserves had swelled to over $38.4 billion — a far cry from the $500 million of reserves in 1991. In 2003, the reserves are in excess of $100 billion. The problem the Reserve Bank of India now faces is managing the huge reserves. In order to discourage short term flows, the Reserve Bank has lowered interest rates and even mandated that the interest paid should not exceed 25 basis points.

Foreign Exchange Risk

This is a real risk and one must be cognizant of the effect of a revaluation or devaluation of the currency either in the home country or in the country the company deals in.

A devaluation in the home country would make the company's products more attractive in other countries. It would also make imports more expensive and if a company is dependent on imports, margins can get reduced. On the other hand, a devaluation in the country to which one exports would make the company's products more expensive and this can adversely impact sales. A method by which foreign exchange risks can be hedged is by entering into forward contracts, i.e. advance purchase or sale of foreign exchange thereby crystallizing the exposure.

In India our currency has been appreciating against the dollar. Thus, the threat investors or recipients of dollars face is that the rupees that they finally receive is less than that they expected. This is an about turn from the situation earlier. As a consequence many have begun quoting in rupees.

Restrictive Practices

Restrictive practices or cartels imposed by countries can affect companies and industries. The United States of America has restrictions regarding the imports of a variety of articles such as textiles. Licenses are given and amounts that may be imported from companies and countries are clearly detailed. Similarly, India has a number of restrictions on what may be imported and at what rate of duty. To an extent this determines the prices at which goods can be sold. If the domestic industry is to be supported, the duties levied may be increased resulting in imports becoming unattractive. During the last two years Indian customs duties have been reduced drastically. Imports are consequently much cheaper and this has affected several industries.

When viewing a company, it is important to see how sensitive it is to governmental policies and restrictive practices.

Foreign Debt and the Balance of Trade

Foreign debt, especially if it is very large, can be a tremendous burden on an economy. India pays around $ 5 billion a year in principal repayments and interest payments. This is no small sum. This has been the price the country has had to pay due to our imports being far in excess of exports and an adverse balance of payments. At the time the country did borrow, it had no alternative. In 1991, at the time of devaluation, India had only enough foreign exchange to finance the imports of few weeks. It is to reverse this that the government did borrow from the World Bank and devalue the currency. A permanent solution will result only when the inflow of foreign currency exceeds the outflow and it is on account of this that tourism, exports and exchange earning/saving industries are encouraged.

Inflation

Inflation has an enormous effect in the economy. Within the country it erodes purchasing power. As a consequence, demand falls. If the rate of inflation in the country from which a company imports is high then the cost of production in that country will automatically go up. This might reduce the cost competitiveness of the product finally manufactured. Conversely, if the rate of inflation in the country to which one exports is high, the products become more attractive resulting in increased sales.

The USA and Europe have fairly low inflation rates (about 5%). In India, inflation has been falling steadily in recent times. It is currently estimated at between 2.5% and 3%. In South America, at one time, it was over 1000%. Money there had no real value. Ironically, South American exports become attractive on account of galloping inflation and the consequent devaluation of their currency which makes their products cheaper in the international markets.

Low inflation within a country indicates stability and domestic companies and industries prosper at such times.

The Threat of Nationalization

The threat of nationalization is a real threat in many countries — the fear that a company may become nationalized. With very few exceptions, nationalized companies are historically less efficient than their private sector counterparts. If one is dependent on a company for certain supplies, nationalization could result in supplies becoming erratic. In addition, the fear of nationalization chokes private investment and there could be a flight of capital to other countries.

Interest Rates

A low interest rate stimulates investment and industry. Conversely, high interest rates result in higher cost of production and lower consumption. When the cost of money is high, a company's competitiveness decreases. In India, the Government has embarked on a drive to have interest rates reduced. This is successful. The interest savings of many companies are significant.

Taxation

The level of taxation in a country has a direct effect on the economy. If tax rates are low, people have more disposable income. In addition they have an incentive to work harder and earn more. And an incentive to invest. This is good for the economy. It is interesting to note that in every economy there is a level between 35% to 55% where tax collection will be the highest. While the tax rates may go up, collection will decline. This is why there it has been argued that the rates in India must be lowered.

Government Policy

Government policy has a direct impact on the economy. A government that is perceived to be pro-industry will attract investment. The liberalization policies of the Narsimha Rao government excited the developed world and foreign companies grew keen to invest in India and increase their existing stakes in their Indian ventures. The move to build and improve infrastructure of the BJP government is creating renewed interest.

Domestic Savings and Its Utilization

If utilized productively, domestic savings can accelerate economic growth. India has one of the largest rate of savings (22%). In USA, it is only 2% whereas in Japan it is as high as 23%. Japan's growth was on account of its domestic savings invested profitably and efficiently. Although India's savings are high, these savings have not been invested either wisely or well. Consequently, there has been little growth. It is to be remembered that all investments are born out of savings. Borrowed funds invested have to be returned. Investments from savings leads to greater consumption in the future. This has been recognized by the Government and it was in order to divert savings to industry the 1992 Finance Act stipulated that productive assets of individuals (shares, debentures, etc.) would not be liable for wealth tax.

The Infrastructure

The development of an economy is dependent on its infrastructure. Industry needs electricity to manufacture and roads to transport goods. Bad infrastructure leads to inefficiencies, poor productivity, wastage and delays. This is possibly the reason why the 1993 budget lay so much emphasis, and offered so many benefits, to infrastructural industries, such as power and transportation. In recent years there has been greater emphasis. Flyovers have been built, national highways are being widened and made better and the improvement made in communications is awesome.

Budgetary Deficit

A budgetary deficit occurs when governmental expenditure exceeds its income. Expenditure stimulates the economy by creating jobs and stimulating demand. However, this can also lead to deficit financing and inflation. Both these, if not checked, can result in spiralling prices. To control and cut deficits governments normally cut governmental expenditure. This would also result in a fall in money supply and a consequent fall in demand which will check inflation. All developing economies suffer from budget deficits as governments spend to improve the infrastructure — build roads, power stations and the like. India is no exception. Budget deficits have been high. The government has, to reduce inflation consciously cut expenditure down and it has reduced from a high of around 15% few years ago to 6% -7% today.

Monsoons

The Indian economy is an agrarian one and it is therefore extremely dependent on the monsoon. Economic activity often comes to a stand still in late March and early April as people wait to see whether the monsoon is likely to be good or not.

Employment

High employment is required to achieve a good growth in national income. As the population growth is faster than the economic growth unemployment is increasing. This is not good for the economy.

Chapter Three

The Economic Cycle

Countries go through the business or economic cycle and the stage of the cycle at which a country is in has a direct impact both on industry and individual companies. It affects investment decisions, employment, demand and the profitability of companies. While some industries such as shipping or consumer durable goods are greatly affected by the business cycle, others such as the food or health industry are not affected to the same extent. This is because in regard to certain products consumers can postpone their purchase decisions, whereas in certain others they cannot.

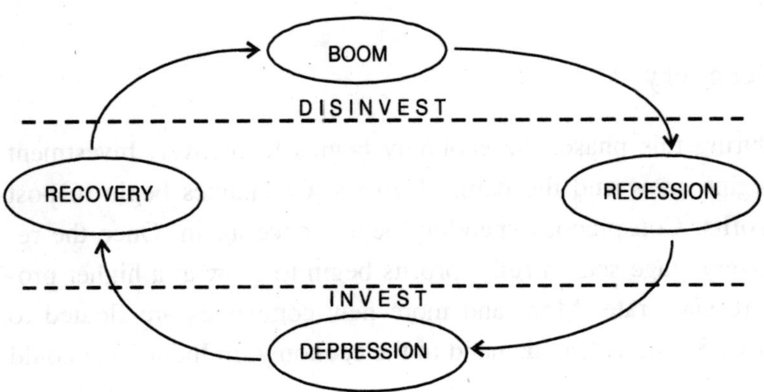

The four stages of an economic cycle are:

- Depression
- Recovery
- Boom
- Recession.

Depression

At the time of depression, demand is low and falling. Inflation is often high and so are interest rates. Companies, crippled by high borrowing and falling sales, are forced to curtail production, close down plants built at times of higher demand, and let workers go.

The United States went through a depression in the late seventies. The economy recovered and the eighties was a period of boom. Another downturn occurred in the late eighties and early nineties, especially after the Gulf War. The recovery of the US economy and that of the rest of Western Europe began again in 1993. Later the US again went through a period of depression at the turn of the millennium. India too went through a difficult period and it began its recovery in 2002.

Recovery

During this phase, the economy begins to recover. Investment begins anew and the demand grows. Companies begin to post profits. Conspicuous spending begins once again. Once the recovery stage sets in fully, profits begin to grow at a higher proportionate rate. More and more new companies are floated to meet the increasing demand in the economy. In India 2003 could be seen as a year of recovery. All the attributes of a recovery are evident in the economy.

Boom

At the boom phase, demand reaches an all time high. Investment is also high. Interest rates are low. Gradually as time goes on, supply begins to exceed the demand. Prices that had been rising begin to fall. Inflation begins to increase.

Recession

The economy slowly begins to downturn. Demand starts falling. Interest rates and inflation begin to increase. Companies start finding it difficult to sell their goods. The economy slowly begins to downturn. Demand starts falling. Interest rates and inflation begin to increase. Companies start finding it difficult to sell their goods. India went through a terrible recession for 4 years from 1996.

The Investment Decision

Investors should attempt to determine the stage of the economic cycle the country is in. They should invest at the end of a depression when the economy begins to recover, and at the end of a recession. Investors should disinvest either just before or during the boom, or, at the worst, just after the boom. Investment and disinvestment made at these times will earn the investor the greatest benefits.

It must however be noted that there is no rule or law that states that a recession would last a certain number of years, or that a boom would be for a definite period of time. Hence the length of previous cycles should not be used as a measure to forecast the length of an existing cycle. An investor should also be aware that government policy or other events can reverse a stage and it is therefore imperative that investors analyze the impact of government and political decisions on the economy before making the final investment decision. Joseph Schumpeter once said, "Cycles are not, like tonsils, separable things that might be treated by themselves but are like the beat of the heart, of the essence of organism that displays them."

Chapter Four

Asset Bubbles

What They Are and How to Protect Yourself When they Burst

An asset bubble occurs when the prices of assets are over-inflated due to an excess of demand. It occurs when there is a lot of money in the system, interest rates are relatively low, credit is easy, unemployment is low. It occurs at a time when economic confidence is high.

Asset bubbles can affect many assets, including commodities, real estate and stocks. At the time of a bubble, there is usually euphoria and a widespread sense of excitement. Price rises are justified by reasoning and the expectation of further increases in price. After several years of a depressed market, prices begin to rise in the wake of an economic boom. Such a relentless price rise was witnessed in the Indian stock markets through 2006 and 2007, finally culminating on 8 January 2008 when the Bombay Stock Exchange Sensitivity Index (Sensex) soared to a high of 21,078. At the time, the euphoria was so great that there were predictions that the Sensex would soar to 50,000 by June 2008. Real estate prices, too, rose in tandem. Credit was easy. Interest rates were relatively low. There was jubilation in the air.

Bubbles burst. When the euphoria becomes unsustainable a crash is inevitable. In the third week of January 2008, the Sensex witnessed great falls. On 21 January 2008, the Sensex fell by 1,408 points. Later, it went into a free fall, falling month on month to close below 9,000 in November 2008. Other assets too fell in sync as demand petered out in the face of an economic depression. There was a similar burst of an asset bubble after the Harshad Mehta scam in 1992-93 and in 2001-2002.

In stock markets, an asset bubble is an extended period of extreme overvaluation. Bubbles occur when there is excessive speculation. As opposed to viewing the intrinsic value of a share (based on fundamental analysis), speculators focus on its resale value. An asset is bought in the expectation that it would double or triple in a relatively short time. Rumours fly. Examples are cited of investors who have made huge killings. Economic data and sensible thought are abandoned for greed. Herd mentality takes over and the mass follow the leader — the bull — without thought or reasoning. In bubbles, it is of no consequence that the price is irrationally high. It only matters that it can be sold for an even higher irrational price at a later date. As happened to the Sensex, bubbles end with steep declines, where most of the speculative gains are quickly wiped out.

The problem is that it is hard to tell a bubble until it bursts. When central or other regulatory bodies intervene, it brings about what it was intended to prevent — a free fall.

There are two types of bubbles.

The first type of asset bubble is created by banks or brokerage houses. They pump up the price of an asset. The assets can be shares, currencies or other financial instruments.

In the second type of bubble, avaricious and susceptible investors are lured into investment swindles by the promise of impossibly high profits and interest payments. In India, the late 1980s and early 1990s witnessed many initial public offerings (IPOs) of investment and other companies which hinted at huge returns and ensnared gullible investors.

When a bubble lasts, a whole host of pundits, analysts and schools try and justify it. I recollect during the Harshad Mehta led boom, pundits justifying it by stating Indian stocks were greatly undervalued and that they had nowhere to go but up. During the boom of 2006-2007, the bubble was justified by saying that the potential of Indian companies was unimaginable — India is the glowing star and the economy is going to grow even faster, went the refrain. People even argued that the new and vibrant economy was exempt from "old rules and archaic modes of thinking". They insisted that productivity had surged and established a steeper but sustainable, trend line. I remember an argument with regard to the valuation of ACC in the early 1990s. The gurus argued that the company should not be valued on the basis of its fundamentals but on what it would cost to build a similar company. The trouble is that these learned people sound authoritative and so sure of themselves that individual investors believe them.

As a fundamental investor, you must be wary of such "This time it's different" arguments. If you cannot understand the reason for the rise in the prices of stocks; if the reason for growth is speculative; if everyone including your maids and taxi drivers are talking of shares, then it would be wise to sell your holdings. I remember in late 2007, a friend wondering when the boom would end and another replying that it would not happen in the foreseeable future. He said it so forcefully that a couple of others sought tips from this individual and bought shares. To their horror, these shares fell by 300% within six months. Also, you must not get carried away by television interviews and newspaper reports. You should remember that these authorities are usually as clueless as you are. If they could actually see the future so clearly, would they be sharing their knowledge with you? They'd be out there making a killing by either selling or buying shares. They are not humanitarians who'd want you to grow wealthy with them.

Claud Cockburn, writing for the *Times of London* from New York described the irrational exuberance that gripped the United States prior to the Great Depression. He wrote: "The atmosphere of the great boom was savagely exciting, but there were times when a person with my European background felt alarmingly lonely. He would have liked to believe, as these people believed, in the eternal upswing of the big bull market or else to meet just one person with whom he might discuss some general doubts without being regarded as an imbecile or a person of deliberately evil intent — some kind of anarchist, perhaps."

The greatest analysts with the most impeccable credentials and track records failed to predict the crash and the unprecedented economic depression that followed it. Newspapers even misled people. On Black Monday (24 October 1929) when the market collapsed The New York Times wrote, "Rally at close cheers brokers, bankers optimistic." Nearer home even our media continues making comments such as this.

Robert Barsky and Bradford De Long wrote in an article entitled "Bull and Bear Markets in the Twentieth Century": "Major bull and bear markets were driven by shifts in assessments of fundamentals; investors had little knowledge of crucial factors, in particular the long run dividend growth rate and their changing expectations of average growth plausibly lie behind the major swings of this century." I agree with this view.

Investments made on hearsay as opposed to those made on the basis of fundamental analysis are doomed from the start. It is shortsighted to buy a share whose intrinsic value is Rs. 30 at Rs. 250 on the expectation that it would grow to Rs. 500 in a year's time. Its intrinsic fundamental value is what it should be purchased at. If its market price is below Rs. 30 buy it, but not if it is any higher.

One bubble burst in 2008. The next bubble may not be far away. You must always beware of this possibility.

Part Two

Industry Analysis

Chapter Five

Industry Analysis

The importance of industry analysis is now dawning on the Indian investor as never before. Previously, investors purchased shares of companies without concerning themselves about the industry it operated in. And they could get away with it three decades ago. This was because India was a sellers' market at that time and products produced were certain to be sold, often at a premium. Those happy days are over. Now, there is intense competition. Consumers have now become quality, cost and fashion conscious. Foreign goods are easily available and Indian goods have to compete with these. There are great technological advances and "state of the art" equipment becomes obsolete in a few years. If not months. In the late 1970s and early 1980s, movie cameras and projectors were prized possessions. With the advent of the video camera in the mid 80s they became obsolete. In 1988, laptop computers were the "in" thing. Everyone raved about the invention and how technology could compress a huge computer into such a small box. These early models did not have a hard disk but two fixed disk drives. A few months later hard disks were incorporated, initially having a capacity of 20 megabytes. The memory was then increased to 40 megabytes. In eighteen months, the laptop became obsolete with the creation of the notebook. These notebooks, some having a capacity of as much as 120 megabytes, are still not the last word in compressed computing. The palm tops have now arrived. Mobile phones today have computing capabilities. One really and honestly does not know what will be next.

I have used these examples to illustrate how technological advances make a highly regarded product obsolete. In the same way, technological advances in one industry can affect another industry. The jute industry went into decline when alternate and cheaper packing materials began to be used. The popularity of cotton clothes in the West affected the manmade (synthetic) textile industry. An investor must therefore examine the industry in which a company operates because this can have a tremendous effect on its results, and even its existence. A company's management may be superior, its balance sheet strong and its reputation enviable. However, the company may not have diversified and the industry within which it operates may be in a depression. This can result in a tremendous decline in revenues and even threaten the viability of the company.

Cycle

The first step in industry analysis is to determine the cycle it is in, or the stage of maturity of the industry. All industries evolve through the following stages:

1. Entrepreneurial, sunrise or nascent stage,
2. Expansion or growth stage,
3. Stabilization, stagnation or maturity stage, and
4. Decline or sunset stage.

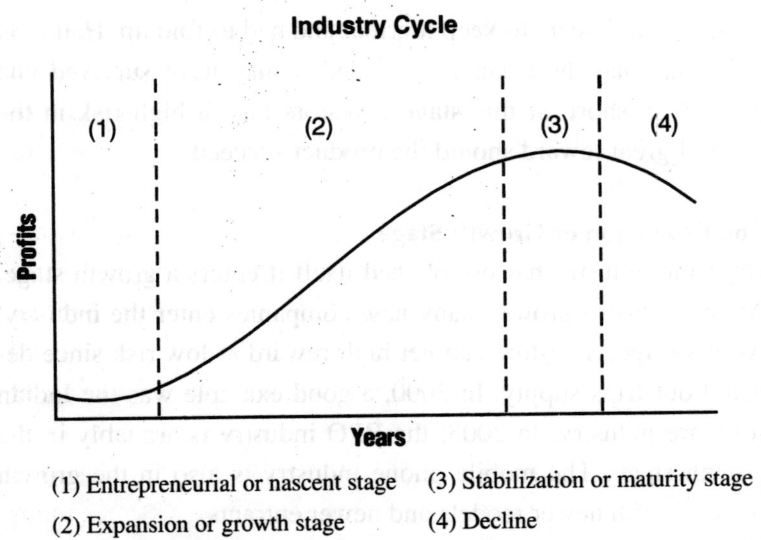

(1) Entrepreneurial or nascent stage (3) Stabilization or maturity stage
(2) Expansion or growth stage (4) Decline

The life cycle of an industry can be illustrated in an inverted "S" curve as illustrated above.

The Entrepreneurial or Nascent Stage

At the first stage, the industry is new and it can take some time for it to properly establish itself. In these early days, it may actually make losses. At this time there may also not be many companies in the industry. It must be noted that the first 5 to 10 years are the most critical period. At this time, companies have the greatest chance of failing. It takes time to establish companies and new products. There may be losses and the need for large injections of capital. If a company or an industry is not nurtured or husbanded at this stage, it can collapse. A good journalist I know began a business magazine. His intention was to start a magazine edited by journalists without interference from industrial magnates or politicians. It was an exceptionally readable magazine. However, it did not have the finance needed in those critical initial years to keep it afloat and had to fold up. Had it, at that time, had the finance it needed it may have survived and thrived. In short, at this stage investors take a high risk in the hope of great reward should the product succeed.

The Expansion or Growth Stage

Once the industry has established itself it enters a growth stage. As the industry grows, many new companies enter the industry. At this stage, investors can get high reward at low risk since demand outstrips supply. In 2000, a good example was the Indian software industry. In 2003, the BPO industry is arguably in the growth stage. The mobile phone industry is also in the growth stage — with newer models and newer entrants.

The growth stage also witnesses product improvements by companies that have survived the first stage. In fact, such companies are often able to even lower their prices. Investors are more keen to invest at this time as companies would have demonstrated their ability to survive.

The Stabilization or Maturity Stage

After the halycon days of growth, an industry matures and stabilizes. Rewards are low and so too is the risk. Growth is moderate. Though sales may increase, they do so at a slower rate than before. Products are more standardized and less innovative and there are several competitors. The refrigerator industry in India is a mature industry. Growth is slow. It is for the time seeing safe. Investors can invest in these industries for comfort and average returns. They must be aware though that should there be a downturn in the economy and a fall in consumer demand, growth and returns can be negative.

The Decline or Sunset Stage

Finally, the industry declines. This occurs when its products are no longer popular. This may be on account of several factors such as a change in social habits (the film and video industry, for example, has suffered on account of cable and satellite television), changes in laws, and increase in prices. The risk at this time is high but the returns are low, even negative.

The various stages can be likened to the four stages in the life cycle of a human being — childhood, adulthood, middle age and old age. Investors should begin to purchase shares when an industry is at the end of the entrepreneurial or nascent stage and during its growth stage, and should begin to disinvest when at its mature stage.

The Industry *vis-a-vis* the Economy

Investors must ascertain how an industry reacts to changes in the economy. Some industries do not perform well during a recession, others exhibit less buoyancy during a boom. On the other hand, certain industries are unaffected in a depression or a boom. What are the major classifications?

1. Industries that are generally unaffected during economic changes are the evergreen industries. These are industries that produce goods individuals need, like the food or agro-based industries (dairy products, etc.)
2. Then there are the volatile cyclical industries which do extremely well when the economy is doing well and do badly when depression sets in. The prime examples are durable goods, consumer goods such as textiles and shipping. During hard times individuals postpone the purchase of consumer goods until better days.

3. Interest sensitive industries are those that are affected by interest rates. When interest rates are high, industries such as real estate and banking fare poorly.
4. Growth industries are those whose growth is higher than other industries and growth occurs even though the economy may be suffering a setback.

What should investors do? Investors should determine how an industry is affected by changes in the economy and movements in interest rates. If the economy is moving towards a recession, investors should disinvest their holdings in cyclical industries and switch to growth or evergreen industries. If interest rates are likely to fall, investors should consider investment in real estate or construction companies. If, on the other hand, the economy is on the upturn, investment in consumer and durable goods industries are likely to be profitable.

Competition

Another factor that one must consider is the level of competition among various companies in an industry. Competition within an industry initially leads to efficiency, product improvements and innovation. As competition increases even more, cut throat price wars set in resulting in lower margins, smaller profits and, finally, some companies begin to make losses. The more inefficient companies even close down.

To properly understand this phenomenon, it is to be appreciated that if the return is high, newcomers will invest in the industry and there will be an inflow of funds. Existing companies may also increase their capacity. However, if the returns are low, or lower than that which can be obtained elsewhere, the reverse will occur. Funds will not be invested and there will be an outflow.

In short high returns attract competition and *vice versa*. However, competition in the form of new companies do not bacterially multiply just because the returns are high. There are competitive forces and it is these competitive forces determine the extent of the inflow of funds, the return on investment and the ability of companies to sustain these returns. These competitive forces are: barriers to entry, the threat of substitution, bargaining power of the buyers, bargaining power of the suppliers, and the rivalry among competitors.

Barriers to Entry

New entrants increase the capacity in an industry and the inflow of funds. The question that arises is how easy is it to enter an industry? There are some barriers to entry:

1. *Economies of Scale*: In some industries it may not be economical to set up small capacities. This is especially true if comparatively large units are already in existence producing a vast quantity. The products produced by such established giants will be markedly cheaper.
2. *Product Differentiation:* A company whose products have product differentiation has greater staying power. The product differentiation may be because of its name or because of the quality of its products — Mercedes Benz cars; National VCRs or Reebok shoes. People are prepared to pay more for the product and consequently the products are at a premium. It is safe usually to invest in such companies as there will always be a demand.
3. *Capital Requirement:* Easy entry industries require little capital and technological expertise. As a consequence, there are a multitude of competitors, intense competition, low margins and high costs. On the other hand, capital intensive industries

with a large capital base and high fixed cost structure have few competitors as entry is difficult. The automobile industry is a prime example of such an industry. Its high fixed costs have to be serviced and a fall in sales can result in a more than proportionate fall in profits. Large investments and a big capital base will be barriers to entry.

4. *Switching Costs:* Another barrier to entry could be the cost of switching From one supplier's product to another. This may include employee retraining costs, cost of equipment and the likes. If the switching costs are high, new entrants have to offer a tremendous improvement for the buyer to switch. A prime example is computers. A company may be using a honeywell computer. If it wishes to change to an IBM computer, all the terminals, the unit and even the software would have to be changed.

5. *Access to Distribution Channels:* Difficulty in securing access to distribution channels can be a barrier to entry, especially if existing firms already have strong and established channels.

6. *Cost Disadvantages Independent of Scale:* This barrier occurs when established firms have advantages new entrants cannot replicate. These include:

   - Proprietary product technology;
   - Favourable access to raw materials;
   - Government subsidies;
   - Long learning curves.

A prime example is Coca Cola. The company has proprietary product technology. Similar cold drinks are available but it is not easy for a competitor to compete with it.

7. *Government Policy:* Government policy can limit fresh entrants to an industry, usually by not issuing licenses. Till about the mid-1980s, the Indian motor car industry was the monopoly of two companies. Even though others sought licenses these were not given.
8. *Expected Retaliation:* The expected retaliation by existing competitors can also be a barrier to potential entrants, especially if existing competitors aggressively try to keep the new entrants out.
9. *Cost of Capacity Additions:* If the cost of capacity additions are high, there will be fewer competitors entering the industry.
10. *International Cartels:* There may be international cartels that make it unprofitable for new entrants.

The Threat of Substitution

New inventions are always taking place and new and better products replace existing ones. An industry that can be replaced by substitutes or is threatened by substitutes is normally an industry one must be careful of investing in. An industry where this occurs constantly is the packaging industry — bottles replaced by cans; cans replaced by plastic bottles, and the like.

To ward off the threat of substitution, companies often have to spend large sums of money in advertising and promotion. The industries that have to worry most are those where the substitutes are either cheaper or better, or are produced by industries earning high profits. It should be noted that substitutes limit the potential returns of a company.

Bargaining Power of the Buyers

In an industry where buyers have control, i.e. in a buyer's market, buyers are constantly forcing prices down, demanding better services or higher quality and this often erodes profitability. The factors one should check are whether

- A particular buyer buys most of the products (large purchase volumes). If such buyers withdraw their patronage, they can destroy an industry. They can also force prices down.
- Buyers can play one company against another to bring prices down.

One should also be aware that:

- If sellers face large switching costs, the buyer's power is enhanced. This is especially true if the switching costs for buyers are low.
- If buyers have achieved partial backward integration, sellers face a threat as they may become fully integrated.
- If buyers are well informed about trends and details they are in a better position *vis-a-vis* sellers as they can ensure they do not pay more than they need to.
- If a product represents a significant portion of the buyers' cost, buyers would strongly attempt to reduce prices.
- If a product is standard and undifferentiated, the buyer's bargaining power is enhanced.
- If the buyer's profits are low, the buyer will try to reduce prices as much as possible.

In short, an industry that is dictated by buyers is usually weak and its profitability is under constant threat.

Bargaining Power of the Suppliers

An industry unduly controlled by its suppliers is also under threat. This occurs when:

- The suppliers have a monopoly, or if there are few suppliers.

- Suppliers control an essential item.
- Demand for the product exceeds supply.
- The supplier supplies to various companies.
- The switching costs are high.
- The supplier's product does not have a substitute.
- The supplier's product is an important input for the buyer's business.
- The buyer is not important to the supplier.
- The supplier's product is unique.

Rivalry Among Competitors

Rivalry among competitors can cause an industry great harm. This occurs mainly by price cuts, heavy advertising, additional high cost services or offers, and the like. This rivalry occurs mainly when:

- There are many competitors and supply exceeds demand. Companies resort to price cuts and advertise heavily in order to attract customers for their goods.
- The industry growth is slow and companies are competing with each other for a greater market share.
- The economy is in a recession and companies cut the price of their products and offer better service to stimulate demand.
- There is a lack of differentiation between the product of one company and that of another. In such cases, the buyer makes his choice on the basis of price or service.
- In some industries economies of scale will necessitate large additions to existing capacities in a company. The increase in production could result in over capacity and price cutting.
- Competitors may have very different strategies in selling their goods and in competing they may be continuously trying to stay ahead of the other by price cuts or improved service.

- Rivalry increases if the stakes (profits) are high.
- Firms will compete with one other intensely if the costs of exit are great, i.e. the payment of gratuity, unfunded provident fund, pension liabilities, and such like. In such a situation, companies would prefer remaining in business even if margins are low and little or no profits are being made. Companies also tend to remain in business at low margins if there are strategic interrelationships between the company and others in the group; due to government restrictions (the government may not allow a company to close down); or in case the management does not wish to close down the company out of pride or employee commitment.

If exit barriers are high, excess capacity can not be shut down and companies lose their competitive edges; profitability is eroded. If exit barriers are high the return is low but risky. If exit barriers are low the return is low but stable. On the other hand, if entry barriers are low the returns are high but stable. High entry barriers have high, risky returns.

Chart 5.1

	High	*Low*
Entry Barriers	Return high but risky	Return high but stable
Exit Barriers	Return low but risky	Return low and stable

Selecting an Industry

When choosing an industry, it would be prudent for the investor to bear in mind or determine the following details:

1. Invest in an industry at the growth stage.

2. The faster the growth of a company or industry, the better. Indian software industry, for example, was growing at a rate of more than 50 per cent per annum at the dawn of the new millennium.
3. It is safer to invest in industries that are not subject to governmental controls and are globally competitive.
4. Cyclical industries should be avoided if possible unless one is investing in them at the time the industry is prospering.
5. Export oriented industries are presently in a favourable position due to various incentives and government encouragement. On the other hand, import substitution companies are presently not doing very well due to relaxations and lower duties on imports.
6. It is important to check whether an industry is right for investment at a particular time. There are sunrise and sunset industries. There are capital intensive and labour intensive industries. Each industry goes through a life cycle. Investments should be at the growth stage of an industry and disinvestment at the maturity or stagnation stage before decline sets in.

Part Three

Company Analysis

At the final stage of fundamental analyses, the investor analysis the company. This analysis has two thrusts:

- How has the company performed *vis-a-vis* other similar companies; and
- How has the company performed in comparison to earlier years?

It is imperative that one completes the politico economic analysis and the industry analysis before a company is analyzed because the company's performance at a period of time is to an extent a reflection of the economy, the political situation and the industry.

What does one look at when analysing a company? There is, in my view, no point or issue too small to be ignored. Everything matters. As I had mentioned earlier, the billionaire Jean Paul Getty, one of the most successful stock market operators of all time, said, "Do not buy a stock until you know all about it."

The different issues regarding a company that should be examined are:

- The Management
- The Company
- The Annual Report
- Ratios
- Cash flow.

Chapter Six

The Management

The single most important factor one should consider when investing in a company, and one often never considered, is its management. It is upon the quality, competence and vision of the management that the future of a company rests. A good, competent management can make a company grow while a weak, inefficient management can destroy a thriving company. Corporate history is riddled with examples. Chrysler was an ailing giant, in the early eighties. Iacocca turned the company round with tough competent management. In the first quarter of 1993, the big blue — IBM — dismissed its Chief Executive Officer Akers who was blamed for the company's dismal performance. Lou Gerstner who was at one time President of American Express and later took charge of R. J. R. Nabisco was invited to become the Chief Executive Officer of IBM. Mr. Gerstner had earlier been successful in reducing quite drastically and very impressively the liabilities that had arisen on account of the leveraged buy out of R. J. R. Nabisco. It was this success that was instrumental in his getting the top job at IBM. Similarly, the main reason attributed for the collapse in the seventies of Penn Central, the largest railway in the United States, was that it was headed by Stuart Saunders who was a lawyer and possessed little understanding of what was involved in running a large railway network. Indian corporate history also has many such examples. Metal Box was a name known and respected, the bluest of blue chips. After a series of occurrences including a diversification that went wrong, the company was forced to close all its factories. Killick Nixon was one of the most respected names in Western India. No longer. On the other hand, there are numerous success stories, of prosperity that resulted due to the foresight and vision of management. Haksar diversified ITC into hotels (the Welcomgroup chain); his successor diversified into agro based industries. These have been successes. The success of Videocon could probably be attributed to Venugopal Dhoot. Bajaj Auto's growth and profitability is due to Rahul Bajaj, and the Reliance Empire due entirely to one man, Dhirubhai Ambani. There are several others such as Azim Premji and Wipro, Narayanamurthy and Infosys and HDFC and Deepak Parekh.

In India, management can be broadly divided into two types:

- Family management;
- Professional management.

Family Management

Family managed companies are those that have at the helm a member of the controlling family. The Chairman or the Chief Executive Officer is usually a member of the "ruling" family and the Board of Directors are peopled either by members of the family or their friends and "rubber stamps". This is not necessarily bad. It is just that all policy is determined by the controlling family and some of the policies may not necessarily always be in the shareholders' best interest. I remember a few years ago Kirloskar Pneumatics was quoting at Rs. 36 per share. At that time

Kirloskar Tractors was not doing well. The controlling family merged the two companies and the price of Kirloskar Pneumatic fell to around Rs. 10. It was probably good for the family and for the shareholders of Kirloskar Tractors but the merger was disastrous for the shareholders of Kirloskar Pneumatics. In short, decisions are often made with family interests in view and employees are often treated as paid servants of the family even though they may be senior managers. For instance, in one company I know the Human Resources Manager is also involved in hiring maids and houseboys for his Chairman's house and he buys the vegetables, too. The New Delhi manager, whenever his "Seth" visits that city is expected to be at the company house every morning at 7 a.m. when the Chairman wakes up, and can only leave his master's presence after he retires for the night. I was witness to an incident at Bombay airport many years ago. The head of a large business house was going on a trip. The chief executives of his many companies had come to see him off. These gentlemen were well known individuals, captains of industry in their own right and respected for their achievements and accomplishments. These leaders bent double and touched their leader's feet when he left, and three of them were actually older than their master. Possibly, this may have been done as a sign of respect like a student touching his teacher's feet, but I do wonder what may have occurred if these individuals had not humiliated themselves with this gesture of obeisance. What I am trying to point out is that in many family run companies, employees are expected to be subservient to the family and loyalty to the family is considered even more important than talent. And often this loyalty is rewarded. If a retainer is ill, he is looked after well and all his medical expenses are borne by the family. When he retires he is given a good pension. I remember an occasion when a senior employee died. His widow was given the company flat, the children were educated and she was even given a job. Few professionally managed or multinationals would do this.

Mr. T. Thomas, a former Chairman of Hindustan Lever Ltd., describes the family business structure most eloquently in his memoir, *To Challenge and to Change*. He speaks of an Indian family business having a series of concentric circles emanating from a core — the core being made up of the founder and his brothers or sons. The next circle is the extended family of cousins and relatives followed by people from the same religious or caste group. The fourth circle comprises of people from the same language group and the outermost circle has people from the same region. Mr. Thomas says that to go beyond this was "like going out of orbit — unthinkably risky"

There has been some change in the way family controlled businesses have been managed. In the beginning, these were often orthodox, autocratic, traditional, rigid and averse to change. This is no longer true. The sons and the grandsons of the founding fathers have been educated at the best business schools in India or abroad and they have been exposed to modern methods. Consequently, in many family managed companies, although the man at the helm is a scion of the family, his subordinates are graduates of business schools, i.e. professional managers. To an extent this combines the best of two worlds and many such businesses are very successful. The frustration for the professional manager in such companies is that he knows that he will never, ever run the company; that privilege will always be with a member of the family.

Professional Management

Professionally managed companies are those that are managed by employees. In such companies, the chief executive officer often does not even have a financial stake in the company. He is at the helm of affairs because of his ability and experience.

The professional manager is a career employee and he remains at the seat of power so long as he meets his targets. Consequently, he is always result-oriented and his aim is often short term — the meeting of the annual budget. He is not necessarily influenced by loyalty to the company. As a professional he is usually aware of the latest trends in management philosophy and tries to introduce these. He tries to run his company like a lean, effective machine striving for increased efficiency and productivity. As a consequence, professionally managed companies are usually well organized, growth oriented and good performers. Investors are the recipients of regular dividends and bonus issues. The companies that come readily to mind are ITC, Infosys, HDFC and Hindustan Lever.

However, there is often a lack of long term commitment and sometimes a lack of loyalty. This is because the professional manager has to step down in time, to retire, and he cannot therefore enjoy the fruit of his labour for ever. Nor will his sons succeed him although some may try to see that this happens. One must also not forget that the professional manager is a mercenary. He sells his services to the highest bidder, and such individuals are consequently not usually known for their loyalty.

Companies now try to promote or create commitment by offering employees stock options. These devolve on employees after a specified period of service and are given to them on performance. The employee thus becomes a part owner and becomes thus involved in the profitability of the enterprise. Additionally as these devolve on the employee only after a time, he tends to stay till it does. As these options are given, often annually, the employee remains with the company for a significant period of time. It is a win-win situation for both. The company gets the services of a loyal competent employee. The employee builds his net worth.

In many professionally managed companies there is also a lot of infighting and corporate politics. This is because managers are constantly trying to climb up the corporate ladder and the end is often what matters, not the means. Often too, as a consequence, the best person does not get the top job; rather, it is the person who plays the game best. This does not always happen in family managed companies as one is aware that the mantle of leadership will always be worn by the son or daughter of the house.

What to Look For

It would be unfair to state that one should invest only in professionally managed companies or family managed companies. There are well managed, profitable companies in both categories. There are also badly managed companies in both categories. What then are the factors one should look for?

1. In my opinion, the most important aspect is the integrity of the management. This must be beyond question. It is often stated that a determined employee can perpetrate a fraud, despite good systems and controls. Similarly, if it so desires, the management can juggle figures and cause great harm and financial loss to a company (for their own personal gain). My recommendation would therefore be to leave a company well alone if you are not too certain of the integrity of its management. I had the privilege once to listen to Mr. C. S. Patel who was at one time the Chief Executive of Unit Trust of India. He re-

counted an advice he was given by his mentor, Mr. A. D. Shroff, the erstwhile Chairman of the New India Assurance: "If you have the slightest doubt of management, do not touch the company with a pair of tongs." Seldom have I heard truer words. When, in a conversation about a company, its management is described colloquially as "*chor* (thief) management", it is a hint to keep well away from that company.

In this context, one should check who the major shareholders of the company are. There are some managements who have a record of manipulating share prices. I was recounted a tale wherein a non Indian journalist asked the scion of a family managed company how he could claim that the share price of his company would not fall below Rs. 230. The worthy replied, "We will not allow it to." Shares of such companies are speculative shares and artificially kept at a high price. They must be avoided.

2. Another point to consider is proven competence, i.e. the past record of the management. How has the management managed the affairs of the company during the last few years? Has the company grown? Has it become more profitable? Has it grown more impressively than others in the same industry?

   It is always wise to be a little wary of new management and new companies as they have a very high level of mortality. Wait until the company shows signs of success and the management proves its competence.

3. How highly is the management rated by its peers in the same industry? This is a very telling factor. Competitors are aware of nearly all the strengths and weaknesses of a management and if they hold the management in high esteem it is truly worthy of respect. It should be remembered that the regard the

industry has of the management of a company is usually impartial, fair and correct.

4. In good times everyone does well. The steel of a management is tested at times of adversity? And during a time of recession or depression, it is important to consider how well the management did? Did it streamline its operations? Did it close down its factories? Did it (if it could) get rid of employees? Was it able to sell its products? Did the company perform better than its competitors? How did sales fare? A management that can steer its company in difficult days will normally always do well.
5. The depth of knowledge of the management, its knowledge of its products, its markets and the industry is of paramount importance because upon this can depend the success of a company. Often the management of a company that has enjoyed a pre-eminent position sits back thinking that it will always be the dominant company. In doing so, it loses its touch with its customers, its markets and its competitors. The reality sinks in only when it is too late. The management must be in touch with the industry and customers at all times and be aware of the latest techniques and innovations. Only then can it progress and keep ahead. A quick way of checking this is to determine what the market share of the company's products is, and whether the share is growing or at least being maintained.
6. The management must be open, innovative and must also have a strategy. It must be prepared to change when required. It must essentially know where it is going and have a plan of how to get there. It must be receptive to ideas and be dynamic. A company that has many layers of management and is top heavy tends to be very bureaucratic and ponderous. There are "many chiefs and few braves". They do not want change and

often stand in the way of change. Their strategy is usually a personal one, on how to hold onto their jobs.

7. I would not recommend investing in a company that is yet to professionalize because in such companies decisions are made on the whims of the chief executive and not with the good of the company in mind. In such companies the most competent are not given the positions of power. There may be nepotism with the nephews, nieces, cousins and relatives of the chief executive holding positions not due to proven competence but because of blood ties.
8. It would be wise, too, to avoid investing in family controlled companies where there is infighting because the companies suffer and the one who arguably stands to lose the most is the shareholder or the investor. In recent years, many such family controlled companies have split, the Birlas, the Goenkas, the Mafatlals, to name but a few. The period before the split and the period soon after are the most unsettled times. That is the time to keep away from such companies. When the new management settles down, one can determine whether one should invest or not.

In India, many of the larger companies are family controlled though they are managed on a day-to-day basis by professional managers. There are also several professionally managed companies. It is not possible, nor would it be fair, to generalize which is better. An investor must, before he risks his money, decide whether he is comfortable with the management of a company. Ultimately, this is what will determine the safety and the fate of the money that you invest.

Chapter Seven

The Company

An aspect not necessarily examined during an analysis of fundamentals is the company. This is because the company is one's perception of the state of a company — it cannot necessarily be supported by hard facts and figures. A company may have made losses consecutively for two years or more and one may not wish to touch its shares — yet it may be a good company and worth purchasing into. There are several factors one should look at.

One of the key factors to ascertain is how a company is perceived by its competitors. Is it held in high regard? The Oscar is Hollywood's greatest award, the one most prized by the stars. Why? It is because it represents recognition of an actor / actress by his / her peers. A company held in scorn by a competitor is not worth looking at. On the other hand, one held in awe must be considered not once but several times. Its products may be far superior. It may be better organized. Its management may be known for its maturity, vision, competence and aggressiveness. The investor must ascertain the reason and then determine whether the reason will continue into the foreseeable future.

Another aspect that should be ascertained is whether the company is the market leader in its products or in its segment When you invest in market leaders, the risk is less. The shares of market leaders do not fall as quickly as those of other companies. There is a magic to their name that would make individuals prefer to buy their products as opposed to others. Let us take a real life example. In the eighties, there was a virtual explosion of consumer goods. There were many television manufacturers. They made similar televisions as almost all parts were imported. However, within a decade only those that were the market leaders survived. The others had died off. If one has to purchase an article and has a choice one would normally buy the better one. This is normal human behaviour and this happens in the market place too. Consequently, the prices of market leaders fall slower than those of others in the same industry.

The policy a company follows is also of imperative importance. What is its plans for growth? What is its vision? Every company has a life. If it is allowed to live a normal life it will grow up to a point and then begin to level out and eventually die. It is at the point of levelling out that it must be given new life. This can give it renewed vigour and a new lease of life. A classic example that comes to mind is ITC Ltd. This tobacco giant branched into hotels under Haksar and then into agribusiness under Sapru. Reliance Industries was initially in Textiles. It then saw opportunity and moved into petroleum, into petro chemicals and refining products. It has in 2003 got into mobile phones. Blue Star is a airconditioning company. It had a software division which was spun off as a separate company. Since then both these companies have grown.

Labour relations are extremely important. A company that has motivated, industrious work force has high productivity and practically no disruption of work. On the other hand, a company that has bad industrial relations will lose several hundred man days as a consequence of strikes and go slows. In 1992 Bata, the giant shoe company, was closed due to strikes for nearly four months and as a consequence its results in the year to 31 March 1993 were extremely bad. It is widely believed that the textile industry died in Mumbai because of the militancy of the unions under the late Datta Samant. It was on account of the militancy of the labour force that many companies grew reluctant to invest in states such as Kerala and West Bengal. It is critical, therefore, to ascertain where the company's plants and factories are and their record of industrial relations.

One must also consider where the company is located and where its factories are. If the infrastructure is bad, if there is inadequate electricity or water the company could have tremendous problems. There are many companies in Madhya Pradesh in dire straits because of electricity cuts. Many cannot afford captive power. Transportation is another issue. The government has recognized this and there are plans afoot to have superhighways around the country within the next ten years.

These are the main factors one should keep at the back of one's mind while viewing a company.

Chapter Eight

The Annual Report

The primary and most important source of information about a company is its Annual Report. By law, this is prepared every year and distributed to the shareholders.

Annual Reports are usually very well presented. A tremendous amount of data is given about the performance of a company over a period of time. Multicoloured bar and pie charts are presented to illustrate and explain the growth of the company and the manner in which the revenues earned have been utilized. There are pictures of the factories; of newly acquired machines; of the Chairman cutting a ribbon and of the Board of Directors looking responsible.

The average shareholder looks no further. If an Annual Report is impressive, if the company has made a profit and if a reasonable dividend has been paid, he is typically content in the belief that the company is in good hands.

This must not be the criteria by which to judge a company. The intelligent investor must read the annual report in depth; he must read between and beyond the lines; he must peep behind the figures and find the truth and only then should he decide whether the company is doing well or not.

The Annual Report is broken down into the following specific parts:

1. The Directors' Report,
2. The Auditor's Report,
3. The Financial Statements, and
4. The Schedules and Notes to the Accounts.

Each of these parts has a purpose and a tale to tell. The tale should be heard.

The Directors' Report

The Directors' Report is a report submitted by the directors of a company to its shareholders, advising them of the performance of the company under their stewardship. It is, in effect, the report they submit to justify their continued existence and it is because of this that these reports should be read with a pinch of salt. After all, if a group of individuals have to present an evaluation of their own performance they are bound to highlight their achievements and gloss over their failures. It is natural. It is human nature. Consequently, all these reports are very well written. Every sentence, nay every word, is subjected to the most piercing scrutiny. Every happening of importance is catalogued and highlighted to convince a casual reader that the company is in good hands. And there is a tendency to justify unhappy happenings. Nevertheless, the Directors' Report provides an investor valuable information:

1. It enunciates the opinion of the directors on the state of the economy and the political situation *vis-a-vis* the company.

2. Explains the performance and the financial results of the company in the period under review. This is an extremely important part. The results and operations of the various separate divisions are usually detailed and investors can determine the reasons for their good or bad performance.
3. The Directors' Report details the company's plans for modernization, expansion and diversification. Without these, a company will remain static and eventually decline.
4. Discusses the profit earned in the period under review and the dividend recommended by the directors. This paragraph should normally be read with sane sckepticism as the directors will always argue that the performance was satisfactory. If profits have improved it would invariably because of superior marketing and hard work in the face of severe competition. If low, adverse economic conditions are usually at fault!.
5. Elaborates on the directors views of the company's prospects in the future.
6. Discusses plans for new acquisitions and investments.

An investor must intelligently evaluate the issues raised in a Directors' Report. Diversification is good but does it make sense? Industry conditions and the management's knowledge of the business must be considered. A diversification in recent times that was a disaster was Burroughs Wellcome's diversification into sport goods, Nike Sportswear in particular. So was Metal Box's move into ball bearings and Spartek's acquisition of Neycer Ceramics. The point I am trying to make is that although companies must diversify in order to spread the risks of industrial slumps, every diversification may not suit a company. Similarly, all other issues raised in the Directors' Report should be analyzed. Did the company perform as well as others in the same industry? Is the finance being raised the most logical and beneficial for the company? It is imperative that the investor read between the lines of Directors' Report and find the answers to these questions.

In short, a Directors' Report is valuable and if read intelligently can give the investor a good grasp of the workings of a company, the problems it faces, the direction it intends takings, and its future prospects.

The Auditor's Report

The auditor represents the shareholders and it is his duty to report to the shareholders and the general public on the stewardship of the company by its directors. Auditors are required to report whether the financial statements presented do, in fact, present a true and fair view of the state of the company. Investors must remember that the auditors are their representative and that they are required by law to point out if the financial statements are not true and fair. They are also required to report any change, such as a change in accounting principles or the non provision of charges that result in an increase or decrease in profits. It is really the only impartial report that a shareholder or investor receives and this alone should spur one to scrutinise the auditor's report minutely. Unfortunately, more often than not it is not read.

There can be interesting contradictions. It was stated in the Auditor's Report of ABC Ltd for the year 2009-2010 that, "As at the year end 31st March 2010, the accumulated losses exceed the net worth of the Company and the Company has suffered cash losses in the financial year ended 31st March 2010 as well as in the immediately preceding financial year. In our opinion, therefore, the Company is a sick industrial company within the meaning of clause (O) of Section 3(1) of the Sick Industrial Companies (Special Provisions) Act 1985". The Directors' report however stated, "The financial year under review has not been a favourable year for the Company as the Computer Industry in general continued to be in the grip of recession. High input costs as well as resource constraints hampered operations. The performance of your Company must be assessed in the light of these factors. During the year manufacturing operations were curtailed to achieve cost effectiveness . . . . Your directors are confident that the efforts for increased business volumes and cost control will yield better results in the current year". The auditors were of the opinion that the company was sick whereas the directors spoke optimistically of their hope that the future would be better! I suppose they could not, being directors, state otherwise.

When reading an Auditor's Report, the effect of their qualification may not be apparent. The Auditor's Report of Royston Electronics Limited for 2009-2010 stated: "In our opinion and to the best of our information and explanation given to us, the said accounts subject to Note No. 3 regarding doubtful debts, No. 4 regarding balance confirmations, No. 5 on custom liability and interests thereon, No 11 on product development expenses, No. 14 on gratuity, No. 8, 16 (C) and 16(F) regarding stocks, give the information in the manner as required by the Companies Act 1956, and give a true and fair view. Let us now look at the specific notes in this case:

1. Note 3 stated that no provision had been made for doubtful debts.
2. It was noted in Note 4 that balance confirmation of sundry debtors, sundry creditors and loans and advances had not been obtained.

3. It was stated in Note 5 that customs liability and interest thereon worth Rs. 3,14,30,073 against the imported raw materials lying in the ICF / Bonded godown as on 31.3.2010 had not been provided.
4. Note 11 drew attention to the fact that product development expenses worth Rs. 17,44,049 were being written off over ten years from 2009-2010. Rs. 2,16,51,023 had been capitalised under this head relating to the development of CT142, Digital TV, Cooler, CFBT which shall be written off in 10 years commencing 2010-11.
5. The company's share towards past gratuity liabilities as of 31 March 2010 had neither been ascertained nor provided for except to the extent of premiums paid against an LIC group gratuity policy taken by the trust (Note 14).
6. Note 16C stated that the raw material consumed had been estimated by the management and this had not been checked by the auditors.

The company made a profit of just over Rs. 1 crore. If the product development expenses, customer duty and interest and provision for bad debts had been made as is required under generally accepted accounting principles, the profit would have turned into a loss.

The point to remember is that at times accounting principles are changed, or creative and innovative accounting practices resorted to by some companies in order to show a better result. The effect of these changes is at times not detailed in the notes to the accounts. The Auditor's Report will always draw the attention of the reader to these changes and the effect that these have on the financial statements. It is for this reason that a careful reading of the Auditor's Report is not only necessary but mandatory for an investor.

Financial Statements

The published financial statements of a company in an Annual Report consist of its Balance Sheet as at the end of the accounting period detailing the financial condition of the company at that date, and the Profit and Loss Account or Income Statement summarizing the activities of the company for the accounting period.

Fundamental Ltd.

Balance Sheet as at 31 March 2010

	2009	*2010*
Sources of Funds		
Shareholders' funds:		
(a) Capital	1,000	1,000
(b) Reserves	8,00	1,650
	1,800	2,650
Loan funds:		
(a) Secured Loans	1,350	1,050
(b) Unsecured Loans	650	500
	2,000	1,550
Total	3,800	4,200
Application of Funds		
Fixed Assets	3,200	3,640
Investments	400	400
Current Assets:		
Trade debtors	600	700
Prepaid Expenses	80	80
Cash and Bank balances	50	100
Other Current Assets	100	150
	830	1,030

Contd . . .

	2009	2010
Less:		
Current Liabilities and provisions		
Trade Creditors	480	710
Accrued Expenses	70	90
Sundry Creditors	80	70
	630	870
Net current assets	200	160
Total	3,800	4,200

Fundamental Ltd.

Profit & Loss Account for the year ended 31 March 2010

	2009	2010
Income		
Sale	14,000	17,500
Other Income	500	600
	14,500	18,100
Expenditure		
Materials	7,600	9,200
Employment	3,450	3,900
Operating and other expenses	1,150	2,100
Interest and finance charges	300	350
Depreciation	80	100
	12,580	15,650
Profit for the year before tax	1,920	2,450
Taxation	900	1,200
	1,020	1,250
Appropriations		
Dividend	220	400
General reserves	200	400
	420	800
Balance carried forward	600	450

Balance Sheet

The Balance Sheet details the financial position of a company on a particular date; of the companys' assets (that which the company owns), and liabilities (that which the company owes), grouped logically under specific heads. It must, however, be noted that the Balance Sheet details the financial position on a particular day and that the position can be materially different on the next day or the day after.

Example: Vasanth Limited had taken a loan of Rs. 200 lakh on 1 December 2009 which was repayable on 1 April 2010. On 31 March 2010, its Balance Sheet was as follows:

Vasanth Ltd.

Balance Sheet as at 31 March 2010

(In Rupees Lakh)

Shareholders' funds	100	Fixed Assets	70
Loan funds	200	Investments	30
Current liabilities	20	Current Assets	220
	320		320

Current assets include cash of Rs. 100 lakh to repay the loan. Vasanth Ltd. did repay the loans, as promised on 1 April 2010. Its Balance Sheet after the repayment read:

Vasanth Ltd.

Balance Sheet as at 1 April 2010

(In Rupees Lakh)

Shareholders' funds	100	Fixed Assets	70
Loan funds	------	Investments	30
Current liabilities	20	Current Assets	20
	120		120

An investor reviewing the Balance Sheets would be forgiven for drawing two very different conclusions. At 31 March 2010, Vasanth Limited would be considered a highly leveraged company, one financed by borrowings. On 1 April 2010, on the other hand, it would be concluded that the company was very conservative and undercapitalized, as a consequence of which its growth would be limited.

Sources of Funds

A company has to source funds to purchase fixed assets, to procure working capital, and to fund its business. For the company to make a profit the funds have to cost less than the return the company earns on their deployment.

Where does a company raise funds? What are the sources?

Companies raise funds from its shareholders and by borrowing.

Shareholders' Funds

A company sources funds from shareholders either by the issue of shares or by ploughing back profits. Shareholders' funds represent the stake they have in the company, the investment they have made.

Share Capital

Share capital represents the shares issued to the public. This is issued in the following ways:

1. *Private Placement*: This is done by offering shares to selected individuals or institutions.
2. *Public Issue*: Shares are offered to the public. The details of the offer, including the reasons for raising the money, are detailed in a prospectus and it is important that investors read

this. Till the scam of 1992 public issues were extremely popular as the shares were often issued to investors at a price much lower than its real value. As a consequence, they were oversubscribed many times. This is no longer true. As companies are now free to price their issues as they like and the office of the controller of capital issues has been abolished, companies typically price their shares at what the market can bear. As a consequence, the investing public are no longer applying blindly for new shares but do so only after a careful analysis.

3. *Rights Issues*: Companies may also issue shares to its shareholders as a matter of right in proportion to their holding. This was often done at a price lower than its market value and shareholders stood to gain enormously. With the new-found freedom in respect of pricing of shares, companies have begun pricing them nearer their intrinsic value. Consequently, these issues have not been particularly attractive to investors and several have failed to be fully subscribed.
4. *Bonus Shares*: Bonus shares are shares issued free to shareholders by capitalizing reserves. No monies are actually raised from shareholders. It can be argued, however, that if these shares are issued by capitalizing distributable reserves, i.e. profits not distributed as dividends, then, in effect, shareholders are contributing capital.

Reserves

Reserves are profits or gains which are retained and not distributed. Companies have two kinds of reserves — capital reserves and revenue reserves:

1. *Capital Reserves*: Capital reserves are gains that have resulted from an increase in the value of assets and they are not freely distributable to the shareholders. The most common capital

reserves one comes across are the share premium account arising from the issue of shares at a premium, and the capital revaluation reserve, i.e. unrealised gain on the value of assets.

2. *Revenue Reserves*: These represent profits from operations ploughed back into the company and not distributed as dividends to shareholders. It is important that all the profits are not distributed as funds are required by companies to purchase new assets to replace existing ones, for expansion, and for working capital.

Loan Funds

The other source of funds a company has access to are borrowings. Borrowing is often preferred by companies as it is quicker, relatively easier and the rules that need to be complied with are less. The loans taken by companies are either:

1. *Secured Loans:* These loans are taken by a company by pledging some of its assets, or by a floating charge on some or all of its assets. The usual secured loans a company has are debentures and term loans.

2. *Unsecured Loans:* Companies do not pledge any assets when they take unsecured loans. The comfort a lender has is usually only the good name and credit worthiness of the company. The more common unsecured loans of a company are fixed deposits and short term loans. In case a company is dissolved, unsecured lenders are usually paid after the secured lenders have been satisfied.

Borrowings or credits for working capital which fluctuate such as bank overdrafts and trade creditors are not normally classified as loan funds but as current liabilities.

Fixed Assets

Fixed assets are assets that a company owns for use in its business and to produce goods, typically, machinery. They are not for resale and comprises of land, buildings, i.e. offices, warehouses and factories, vehicles, machinery, furniture, equipment and the like.

Every company has some fixed assets though the nature or kind of fixed assets vary from company to company. A manufacturing company's major fixed assets would be its factory and machinery, whereas that of shipping company would be its ships.

Fixed assets are shown in the Balance Sheet at cost less the accumulated depreciation. Depreciation is based on the very sound concept that an asset has a useful life and that after years of toil it wears down. Consequently, it attempts to measure the wear and tear and to reduce the value of the asset accordingly so that at the end of its useful life, the asset will have no value. As depreciation is a charge on profits, at the end of its useful life, the company would have set aside from profits an amount equal to the original cost of the asset and this could be utilised to purchase another asset. However, in these inflationary times, this is inadequate and some companies create an additional reserve to ensure that there are sufficient funds to replace the worn out asset. The common methods of depreciation are:

1. *Straight Line Method:* The cost of the asset is written off equally over its life. Consequently, at the end of its useful life, the cost will equal the accumulated depreciation.
2. *Reducing Balance:* Under this method, depreciation is calculated on the written down value, i.e. cost less depreciation. Consequently, depreciation is higher in the beginning and

lower as the years progress. An asset is never fully written off as the depreciation is always calculated on a reducing balance.

3. Others: There are a few others such as the interest method and the rate of 72 but these are not commonly used.

Land is the only fixed asset that is never depreciated as it normally appreciates in value. Capital work in progress — factories being constructed, etc. — is not depreciated until it is a fully functional asset.

Investments

Many companies purchase investments in the form of shares or debentures to earn income or to utilize cash surpluses profitably. The normal investments a company has are:

1. *Trade:* Trade investments are shares or debentures of competitors that a company holds to have access to information on their growth, profitability and other details which may not, otherwise, be easily available.
2. *Subsidiary and Associate Companies:* These are shares held in subsidiary or associate companies. The large business houses hold controlling interest in several companies through cross holdings in subsidiary and associate companies.
3. *Others:* Companies also often hold shares or debentures of other companies for investment or to park surplus funds. The windfall profits made by many companies in the year to 31 March 2003 was on account of the large profits made by trading in shares.

Investments are also classified as quoted and unquoted investments. Quoted investments are shares and debentures that are quoted in a recognized stock exchange and can be freely traded. Unquoted investments are not listed or quoted in a stock exchange. Consequently, they are not very liquid and are difficult to dispose of.

Investments are valued and stated in the balance sheet at either the acquisition cost or market value, whichever is lower, in order to be conservative and to ensure that losses are adequately accounted for.

Current Assets

Current assets are assets owned by a company which are used in the normal course of business, or are generated by the company in the course of business, such as debtors or finished stock or cash. The rule of thumb is that any asset that is turned into cash within twelve months is a current asset.

Current assets can be divided essentially into three categories:

1. *Converting Assets:* Assets that are produced or generated in the normal course of business, such as finished goods and debtors.
2. *Constant Assets:* Constant assets are those that are purchased and sold without any add ons or conversions, such as liquor bought by a liquor store from a liquor manufacturers.
3. *Cash Equivalents:* These are assets that are in the form of cash or cash equivalents. They can be used to repay dues or purchase other assets. The most common cash equivalent assets are cash in hand and at the bank, and loans given.

The current assets a company has are:

Stock or Inventories

These are arguably the most important current assets that a company has as it is by the sale of its stocks that a company makes its profits. Stocks, in turn, consist of:

1. *Raw Materials:* The primary purchase which is utilised to manufacture the products a company makes.
2. *Work in Progress:* Goods that are in the process of manufacture but are yet to be completed.
3. *Finished Goods:* The finished products manufactured by the company that are ready for sale

Valuation of Stocks

Stocks are valued at the lower of cost or net realizable value. This is to ensure that there will be no loss at the time of sale as that would have been accounted for.

The common methods of valuing stocks are:

1. *FIFO or First in First Out*: It is assumed under this method that stocks that come in first would be sold first and those that come in last would be sold last.
2. *LIFO or Last in Last Out*: The premise on which this method is based is the opposite of FIFO. It is assumed that the stocks that arrive last will be sold first. The reasoning is that customers prefer newer materials or products.

It is important to ascertain the method of valuation and the accounting principles involved as stock values can easily be manipulated by changing the method of valuation.

Trade Debtors

Most companies do not sell their products for cash but on credit and purchasers are expected to pay for the goods they have bought within an agreed period of time, 30 days or 60 days. The period of credit would vary from customer to customer and from company to company and depends on the credit worthiness of the customer, market conditions and competition.

Often customers may not pay within the agreed credit period. This may be due to laxity in credit administration or the inability of the customers to pay. Consequently, debts are classified as:

- those over six months; and
- others.

These are further subdivided into:

- debts considered good; and
- debts considered bad and doubtful.

If debts are likely to be bad, they must be provided for or written off. If this is not done assets will be overstated to the extent of the bad debt. A write off is made only when there is no hope of recovery. Otherwise, a provision is made. Provisions may be specific or they may be general. When amounts are provided on certain identified debts, the provision is termed specific whereas if a provision amounting to a certain percentage of all debts are made, the provision is termed general.

Prepaid Expenses

All payments are not made when due. Many payments, such as insurance premiums, rent and service costs, are made in advance for a period of time which may be 3 months, 6 months, or even a year. The portion of such expenses that relates to the next accounting period are shown as prepaid expenses in the Balance Sheet.

Cash and Bank Balances

Cash in hand in petty cash boxes, tills, safes, and balances in bank accounts are shown under this heading in the Balance Sheet.

Loans and Advances

These are loans that have been given to other corporations, individuals and employees and are repayable within a certain period of time. This also includes amounts paid in advance for the supply of goods, materials and services.

Other Current Assets

Other current assets are all amounts due that are recoverable within the next twelve months. These include claims receivable, interest due on investments and the like.

Current Liabilities

Current liabilities are amounts due that are payable within the next twelve months. These also include provisions which are amounts set aside for an expense incurred for which the bill has not been received as yet or whose cost has not been fully estimated.

Trade Creditors

Trade creditors are those to whom the company owe monies for raw materials and other articles used in the manufacture of its products. Companies usually purchase these on credit, the credit period depending on the demand for the item, the standing of the company and market practice.

Accrued Expenses

Certain expenses such as interest on bank overdrafts, telephone costs, electricity and overtime are paid after they have been incurred. This is because they fluctuate and it is not possible to either prepay or accurately anticipate these expenses. However, the expense has been incurred. To recognize this, the expense incurred is estimated, based on past trends and known expenses incurred and accrued on the date of the Balance Sheet.

Provisions

Provisions are amounts set aside from profits for an estimated expense or loss. Certain provisions such as depreciation and provisions for bad debts are deducted from the concerned asset itself. There are others, such as claims that may be payable, for which provisions are made. Other provisions normally seen on balance sheets are those for dividends and taxation.

Sundry Creditors

Any other amounts due are usually clubbed under the all embracing title of sundry creditors. These include unclaimed dividends and dues payable to third parties.

Profit and Loss Account

The Profit and Loss account summarizes the activities of a company during an accounting period which may be a month, a quarter, six months, a year, or longer, and the result achieved by the company. It details the income earned by the company, its costs and the resulting profit or loss. It is, in effect, the performance appraisal not only of the company but also of its management — its competence, foresight and ability to lead.

Sales

Sales is the amount received or receivable from customers arising from the sales of goods and the provision of services by a company. A sale occurs when the ownership of goods and the consequent risk relating to these goods are passed to the customer in return for consideration, usually cash. In normal circumstances the physical possession of the goods is also transferred at the same time. A sale does not occur when a company places goods at the shop of a dealer with the clear understanding that payment need be made only after the goods are sold failing which they may be returned. In such a case, the ownership and risk are not transferred to the dealer nor any consideration paid.

Companies do give trade discounts and other incentive discounts to customers to entice them to buy their products. Sales should be accounted for after deducting these discounts. However, cash discounts given for early payment are a finance expense and should be shown as an expense and not deducted from sales.

There are many companies which deduct excise duty and other levies from sales. There are others who show this as an expense. It is preferable to deduct these from sales since the sales figure would then reflect the actual markup made by the company on its cost of production.

Other Income

Companies may also receive income from sources other than from the sale of their products or the provision of services. These are usually clubbed together under the heading, other income. The more common items that appear under this title are:

1. *Profit from the Sale of Assets*: Profit from the sale of investments or assets.

2. *Dividends*: Dividends earned from investments made by the company in the shares of other companies.
3. *Rent*: Rent received from commercial buildings and apartments leased from the company.
4. *Interest:* Interest received on deposits made and loans given to corporate and other bodies.

Materials

Materials are the raw materials and other items used in the manufacture of a company's products. It is also sometimes called the cost of goods sold.

Employment Costs

The costs of employment are accounted for under this head and would include wages, salaries, bonus, gratuity, contributions made to provident and other funds, welfare expenses, and other employee related expenditure.

Operating and Other Expenses

All the costs incurred in running a company are called operating and other expenses, and include:

1. *Selling Expenses:* The cost of advertising, sales commissions, sales promotion expenses and other sales related expenses.
2. *Administration Expenses:* Rent of offices and factories, municipal taxes, stationery, telephone and telex costs, electricity charges, insurance, repairs, motor maintenance, and all other expenses incurred to run a company.

3. *Others*: This includes costs that are not strictly administration or selling expenses, such as donations made, losses on the sale of fixed assets or investments, miscellaneous expenditure and the like.

Interest and Finance Charges

A company has to pay interest on monies it borrows. This is normally shown separately as it is a cost distinct from the normal costs incurred in running a business and would vary from company to company. The normal borrowings that a company pays interest on are:

1. Bank overdrafts,
2. Term loans taken for the purchase of machinery,
3. Fixed deposits from the public,
4. Debentures, and
5. Intercorporate loans.

Depreciation

Depreciation represents the wear and tear incurred by the fixed assets of a company, i.e. the reduction in the value of fixed assets on account of usage. This is also shown separately as the depreciation charge of similar companies in the same industry will differ, depending on the age of the fixed assets and the cost at which they have been bought.

Taxation

Most companies are taxed on the profits that they make. It must be remembered however, that taxes are payable on the taxable income or profit and this can differ dramatically from the accounting income or profit. This is because many amounts legitimately expensed may not be tax deductible. Conversely, income such as agricultural income is not taxable.

Dividends

Dividends are profits distributed to shareholders. The total profits after tax are not always distributed; a portion is often ploughed back into the company for its future growth and expansion. Dividends paid during the year in anticipation of profits are known as interim dividends. The final dividend is usually declared after the results for the period have been determined. The final dividend is proposed at the annual general meeting of the company and paid after the approval of the shareholders.

Transfer to Reserves

The transfer to reserves is the profit ploughed back into the company. This may be done to finance working capital, expansion, fixed assets or for some other purpose. These are revenue reserves and can be distributed to shareholders as dividends.

Contingent Liabilities

Contingent liabilities are liabilities that may arise up on the happening of an event. It is uncertain, however, whether the event itself may happen. This is why these are not provided for and shown as an actual liability in the balance sheet. Contingent liabilities are detailed in the Financial Statements as a note to inform the readers of possible future liabilities while arriving at an opinion about the company. The contingent liabilities one normally encounters are:

- Bills discounted with banks — these may crystallize into active liabilities if the bills are dishonoured.
- Gratuity to employees not provided for.
- Legal suits against the company not provided for.
- Claims against a company not acknowledged or accepted.
- Excise claims against the company.

Schedules and Notes to the Accounts

The schedules and notes to the accounts are an integral part of the financial statements of a company and it is important that they be read along with the financial statements. Most people avoid reading these. They do so at their own risk as these provide vital clues and information.

Schedules

The schedules detail pertinent information about the items of Balance Sheet and Profit & Loss Account. It also details information about sales, manufacturing costs, administration costs, interest, and other income and expenses. This information is vital for the analysis of financial statements. The schedules enable an investor to determine which expenses increased and seek the reasons for this. Similarly, investors would be able to find out the reasons for the increase or decrease in sales and the products that are sales leaders. The schedules even give details of stocks and sales, particulars of capacity and productions, and much other useful information.

Notes

The notes to the accounts are even more important than the schedules because it is here that very important information relating to the company is stated. Notes can effectively be divided into:

1. Accounting Policies,
2. Contingent Liabilities, and
3. Others.

Accounting Policies

All companies follow certain accounting principles and these may differ from those of other entities. As a consequence, the profit earned might differ. Companies have also been known to change (normally increase) their profit by changing the accounting policies. For instance, Tata Iron and Steel Company's Annual Report for 1991-92 stated among other things, "There has been a change in the method of accounting relating to interest on borrowings used for capital expenditure. While such interest was fully written off in the previous years, interest charges incurred during the year have been capitalised for the period up to the date from which the assets have been put to use. Accordingly, expenditure transferred to capital account includes an amount of Rs. 46.63 crore towards interest capitalised. The profit before taxes for the year after the consequential adjustments of depreciation of Rs. 0.12 crore is therefore higher by Rs. 46.51 crore than what it would have been had the previous basis been followed". This means that by changing an accounting policy, TISCO was able to increase its income by Rs. 46 crore. There could be similar notes on other items in the financial statements.

The accounting policies normally detailed in the notes relate to:

1. How sales are accounted.
2. What the research and development costs are.

3. How the gratuity liability is expensed.
4. How fixed assets are valued.
5. How depreciation is calculated.
6. How stock, including finished goods, work in progress, raw materials and consumable goods are valued.
7. How investments are stated in the balance sheet.
8. How has the foreign exchange translated?

Contingent Liabilities

As noted earlier, contingent liabilities are liabilities that might crystallize upon the happening of an uncertain event. All contingent liabilities are detailed in the notes to the accounts and it would be wise to read these as they give valuable insights. The more common contingent liabilities that one comes across in the financial statements of companies are:

1. Outstanding guarantees.
2. Outstanding letters of credit.
3. Outstanding bills discounted.
4. Claims against the company not acknowledged as debts.
5. Claims for taxes.
6. Cheques discounted.
7. Uncalled liability on partly paid shares and debentures.

Others

It must be appreciated that the purpose of notes to the accounts is to inform the reader more fully. Consequently, they detail all pertinent factors which affect, or will affect, the company and its results. Often as a consequence, adjustments may need to be made to the accounts to unearth the true results.

Note 6 of Fundamental & Co. Ltd.'s Annual Report for 2009-2010 stated: "The Company has during the year credited an amount of Rs. 132.14 lakh to surplus on sale of assets (Schedule

No. 13) which included an amount of Rs. 112.88 lakh being the excess of sale price over the original cost of the fixed assets. Till the accounting year 2008-2009, such excess over the original cost was credited to capital reserve. Had the Company followed the earlier method of accounting the profit for the year would have been lower by Rs. 112.88 lakh." This suggests that the company had changed its accounting policy in order to increase its profits. The profit before tax that year (year ended 31 March 2010) was Rs. 108.12 lakh (previous year Rs. 309.80 lakh). Had this adjustment not been made, the company would have suffered a loss of Rs. 4.76 lakh. The company had also withdrawn Rs. 35.34 lakh from the revaluation reserve. It was also stated in that company's annual report that "no provision had been made for Rs. 16.39 lakh being the fall in the break-up value of unquoted shares in wholly owned subsidiary companies" and "the income tax liability amounting to Rs. 36.41 lakh relating to prior years has been adjusted against the profits transferred to the General Reserve in the respective years". The latter points out that the tax charge had been adjusted directly with reserves as opposed to routing it through the Profit and Loss account. Had that been done the profit after tax would have further reduced. Similar comments are made in the notes to the accounts of other companies also.

The more common notes one comes across are:

1. Whether provisions for known or likely losses have been made.
2. Estimated value of contracts outstanding.
3. Interest not provided for.
4. Arrangements agreed by the company with third parties.
5. Agreements with labour.

The importance of these notes cannot be overstressed. It is imperative that investors read these carefully.

Chapter Nine

Ratios

No person should invest in a company until he has analyzed its financial statements and compared its performance to what it achieved in the previous years, and with that of other companies. This can be difficult at times because:

1. The size of the companies may be different.
2. The composition of a company's balance sheet may have changed significantly. It may have issued shares, or increased or reduced borrowings.

It is in the analysis of financial statements that ratios are most useful because they help an investor to compare the strengths, weaknesses and performance of companies and to also determine whether it is improving or deteriorating in profitability or financial strength.

Ratios express mathematically the relationship between performance figures and / or assets / liabilities in a form that can be easily understood and interpreted. Otherwise, one may be confronted by a battery of figures that are difficult to draw meaningful conclusions from. It should be noted that figures by themselves do not enable one to arrive at a conclusion about a company's strength or performance. Sales of Rs. 500 crore a year or a profit of Rs. 200 crores in a year may appear impressive but one cannot be impressed until this is compared with other figures, such as the company's assets or net worth or capital employed. It is also important to focus on ratios that are meaningful and logical. Otherwise, no useful conclusion can be arrived at. A ratio expressing sales as a percentage of trade creditors or investments is meaningless as there is no commonality between the figures. On the other hand, a ratio that expresses the gross profit as a percentage of sales indicates the mark up on cost or the margin earned.

No Single Ratio Tells the Complete Story

There is no point in computing just one ratio as it will not give the whole picture but just one aspect. It is only when the various different ratios are calculated and arranged that the complete state of a company emerges and it is important that an investor has as much information as possible before he actually invests.

Ratios can be broken down into four broad categories:

Profit and Loss Ratios

These show the relationship between two items or groups of items in a profit and loss account or income statement. The more common of these ratios are:

1. Sales to cost of goods sold,
2. Selling expenses to sales,
3. Net profit to sales, and
4. Gross profit to sales.

Balance Sheet Ratios

These deal with the relationship in the balance sheet such as:

1. Shareholders' equity to borrowed funds,

2. Current assets to current liabilities,
3. Liabilities to net worth,
4. Debt to assets, and
5. Liabilities to assets.

Balance Sheet and Profit and Loss Account Ratios

These relate an item on the balance sheet to another in the profit and loss account such as:

1. Earnings to shareholders' funds.
2. Net income to assets employed.
3. Sales to stock,
4. Sales to debtors, and
5. Cost of goods sold to creditors.

Financial Statements and Market Ratios

These are normally known as market ratios and are arrived at by relating financial figures to market prices:

1. Market value to earnings, and
2. Book value to market value.

In this book, ratios have been grouped into eight categories that will enable an investor to easily determine the strengths or weaknesses of a company.

1. Market Value
2. Earnings
3. Profitability
4. Liquidity
5. Leverage
6. Debt Service Capacity
7. Asset Management/Efficiency
8. Margins.

Of course, it must be ensured that the ratios being measured are consistent and valid. The length of the periods being compared should be similar. Large non-recurring income or expenditure should be omitted when calculating ratios calculated for earnings or profitability, otherwise the conclusions will be incorrect.

Ratios do not provide answers. They suggest possibilities. Investors must examine these possibilities along with general factors that would affect the company, such as its management, management policy, government policy, the state of the economy and the industry to arrive at a logical conclusion and he must act on such conclusions.

Ratios are a terrific tool for interpreting financial statements but their usefulness depends entirely on their logical and intelligent interpretation.

Market Value

Ultimately the market value of a share is what matters to an investor. An investor would purchase a share if, in his perception, its price is low or reasonable and has growth potential. On the other hand, if a share is priced high an investor would want to sell it. After all, the cardinal rule of investment in shares is to buy cheap, sell dear or, as Baron Rothschild is credited to have said, "Buy sheep and sell deer." Additionally, the market value of a share reflects the regard investors and the general public have of the company.

Market value ratios also help an investor determine the length of time it would take to recover his or her investment.

Price-Earnings Ratio

The Price-Earnings or P/E ratio is arguably the most commonly quoted ratio. Investors, analysts and advisers alike quote this ratio to justify or support their contention. The reason for its popularity is that it reduces to an arithmetical figure the relationship between market price and the earnings per share and thereby allows one the opportunity to determine whether a share is overpriced or under priced and check the time it would take to recover one's investment. In addition, it reflects the opinion of the investing public about the company, i.e. whether the company is growing or declining, and whether the price is likely to rise, fall or remain stagnant.

The P/E ratio is calculated by dividing the market price of a company's share by its earning's per share, i.e. profit after tax and preference dividend divided, by the number of shares issued by the company.

$$\text{Price-Earnings Ratio} = \frac{\text{Market price per share}}{\text{Earnings per share}}$$

Samudra Lamps Ltd is a company involved in the manufacture of electric bulbs and tube lights. At 31 March, its shareholders funds were as follows:

	(Rs. lakh)
500,000 shares of Rs. 10 each	50
100,000 10% preference shares of Rs. 10 each	10
Reserves	70
	130

The profit that the company made that year after tax and preference dividend was Rs. 400 lakh. The market price of the share on 31 March was Rs. 112.

The earnings per share would be:	400 ÷ 50 =	Rs. 8
The price earnings ratio would be:	112 ÷ 8 =	Rs.14

This means that the investor would take 14 years to recover his investment through earnings.

This also translates to a yield of 7.14% (100/14 years).

The P/E ratios of well established and financially sound companies are high and as the returns are high for weaker companies the P/E ratio is low since they are riskier investments.

The P/E ratio would be high so long as the investing public has faith in a company's ability to grow and to earn a return or an appreciation in its share price. It will fall as soon as this confidence in the earning capacity of the company falls. This is why prices rise dramatically in boom periods. In periods of depression, they fall.

The price an investor pays for a share is based on the future prospects of a company and its anticipated earnings. As such, there is a flaw in P/E ratios when current market price is divided by past earnings per share. Ideally, the current market price should be divided by the current likely earnings per share. But then that figure is difficult to get.

The P/E ratio reflects the reputation of the company and its management and the confidence investors have in the earning potential of the company.

An investor may well ask what should be the P/E ratio of a company; at what price should one purchase the share of a company. At the height of the 1992 scam in India, the P/E of several companies such as Hindustan Lever Ltd, ITC Ltd., etc. were in excess of 100! The average P/E of companies quoted on the Bombay Stock Exchange averaged 80. Even a year after the scam the average P/E was around 37. This was one of the widely-cited reasons for foreign investors not descending in droves on the Indian stock markets. It was argued that the average P/E of shares in developed economies like the United States was then around 20. This offered a yield of 5% which was about 2% above the rate of inflation. On that basis, if one assumed that the rate of inflation in India is around 10%, then the P/E of shares one wished to purchase should be 8. This would result in a yield of 12.5% which would be 2.5% above the rate of inflation. As inflation falls, the P/E will rise and the yield will fall. In a country like India, interest rates have begun to fall dramatically. What should the P/E be now. I'd like to introduce, at this juncture, a school of thought promoted by those I term the developing economy proponents. They argue that the average P/E of shares in developing economies, i.e. in countries in South East Asia, average 45. They claim that P/Es have to be higher in developing economies as companies are growing and the high P/Es reflect this growth. As companies mature, earnings will stabilize and the P/Es fall.

That may be so. In my opinion, though, I feel that in India it would be safer for investors to buy shares of companies that have a relatively lower P/E between 11 and 13. One should think twice before purchasing a share that has a higher P/E.

Having said that, the P/E that different investors would be prepared to accept as reasonable would depend on:

1. The company and their perception of its management, growth, prospects, and the industry it operates in;
2. The demand for the shares of the company. Certain companies such as ITC, Reliance, etc. have rewarded their investors well over the years and these shares command higher P/Es.
3. The profitability and earnings of a company.
4. The target returns of different investors.

In short, the P/E that is considered reasonable by different investors will be the one that fulfils their particular investment return requirement.

The pricing of shares as far as P/E is concerned lost all meaning in 1999 with respect to IT shares. Companies such as Amazon.com and many others that were loss making were quoting at P/E ratios that made no sense. The basis was on perceived earnings, projected earnings and potential earnings not actual earnings. In such a situation one's guess or price was good as the others.

Market to Book Ratio

The market to book ratio compares the book value of the assets of a company to its market value. If a share's market price is treble or quadruple its book value, it signifies that investors have tremendous confidence in the growth prospects of the company. It can also suggest that the assets may be understated. If, on the other hand, the book value is more than the market value, the company may not be making profits and may not be enjoying investor confidence. The market to book ratio is calculated by dividing the market price per share by the book value per share.

$$\text{Market to book ratio} = \frac{\text{Market price per share}}{\text{Book value per share}}$$

For example, if the market price of the shares of Mithawala Chemicals Ltd. is Rs. 105 and the book value of its shares is Rs. 48, its market to book ratio is 105/48 = 2.1875.

The market value of the shares of Mithawala Chemicals is more than twice its book value. This suggests that either the assets of the company are understated or its prospects are good and that investors believe that it will grow in income, value and profitability.

As a rule of thumb, one should not purchase a share which is priced more than thrice its book value because the gap is enormous and the difference would not be backed by tangible assets. As a consequence, there could be a big fall in the price.

Table 9.1

Market to Book Value of Certain Selected Companies

Name of the Company	*Book Value as on 31-03-2010*	*Market Value as on 11 June, 2010*
ACC	320.11	855.00
Asian Paints	194.35	2288.50
Bajaj Auto	246.73	2306.00
Axis Bank	394.31	1239.80
State Bank of India	1057.10	2322.00
Cipla	67.61	337.05
HDFC	453.61	2796.00
GE Shipping	349.59	297.25
Hindalco	134.27	139.55
HPCL	355.31	347.75
Indian Hotels	44.25	100.40
IDFC	54.18	162.40
ITC	46.18	282.00
Infosys Technologies	384.22	2645.90
Oracle Financial Services	418.47	2170
M&M	93.61	603.20
Hexaware	52.84	75.45
HDFC Bank	470.79	1937.10
Nirma Ltd.	180.40	178.39
ONGC	446.51	1184.50
Reliance Industries Ltd.	392.51	1046.00
SAIL	84.10	196.50
Tata Motors	217.77	761.20
Biocon	81.11	302.10
Kotak Mahindra Bank	128.35	753.40
Glenmark Pharma	50.41	258.35

Let me illustrate the differences between market and book value in a few companies (*See* Table 9.1). There are large differences between the market value and the book value.

Summary

The market value ratios are extremely important because these determine an investment decision. If one remembers, as technical analysts would vouch, that the market price of a share takes into account the profitability, earnings, prospects and all other aspects of a company, market ratios go on to another dimension — as the only ratios that evaluate the price of a share for an investor to determine whether it is under priced or overpriced.

Earnings

Earnings is the yardstick by which companies are finally judged, namely what investors earn on their investments. The earnings ratios are often used to determine the fair market price of a share and to value investments.

As a consequence, these are the most important ratios for investors and it is important that they be appreciated and understood.

Earnings per Share

The earnings per share (EPS) ratio indicates the earning of a common share in a year. This ratio enables investors to actually quantify the income earned by a share, and to determine whether it is reasonably priced. The ratio is arrived at by dividing the income attributable to common shareholders by the weighted average of common shares:

$$\text{Earnings per share} = \frac{\text{Income attributable to common shareholders}}{\text{Weighted average number of common shares}}$$

Illustration

In 2008, the earnings after tax of Range View Tea Estates was Rs. 5,00,000. Between 1 January 2010 and 30 June 2010 the company had 200,000 shares of Rs. 10 each outstanding. On 1 July 2010, the company issued an additional 100,000 shares.

The earnings per share of Range View would be:

$$\frac{500,000}{[\,200.000 \times 0.5 + (300,000 \times 0.5)\,]} = \text{Rs. } 2$$

In countries including India where employees are given stock options, investors check a company's fully diluted earnings per share. This is the earnings per share of a company after all share options, warrants and convertible securities outstanding at the end of the accounting period are exchanged for shares.

Many investors also value a share as a multiple of the earnings of the company. If the earning per share is Rs. 5 and a yield of 10% is considered reasonable, the share is priced at Rs. 50.

Cash Earnings per Share

It is often argued that the earnings per share is not a proper measure of the earning of a company since depreciation, tax and the cost of finance varies from one company to another. The true earnings, the argument goes on, should be calculated on the earning before depreciation, interest and tax. The cash earning per share is arrived at by dividing earning before depreciation, interest and tax (EDBIT) by the weighted average number of shares issued.

The cash earnings per share will always be more than the earnings per share.

$$\text{Cash earnings per share} = \frac{\text{EDBIT}}{\text{Weighted average number of shares issued}}$$

Illustration

The summarised Profit and Loss Account (Income Statement) of Nikhila Chips Ltd. for the latest financial year was as follows:

	Rs. (lakh)	*Rs. (lakh)*
Sales		5,000
Cost of goods sold		3,000
Gross Income		2,000
Selling costs	300	
*Administration Expenses	200	500
Net Income		Rs. 1,500

*Administration expenses includes interest costs of Rs. 40 and depreciation of Rs. 20.

The company had issued 500,000 shares of Rs. 10 each.

The cash earning of a share in Nikhila Chips Ltd. would therefore be:

$$\frac{1500+40+20}{500} = \text{Rs. } 3.12$$

Dividend per Share

Investors often use the dividend per share as a measure to determine the real value of a share. Proponents of this school of thought argue that the earning per share is of no real value to anyone but those who can determine the policies of a company. The income of an investor is the dividend that he receives. It is therefore submitted that the value of a share should be a multiple of the dividend paid on that share.

How does one value a share? If one assumes that the gains made by an investor would include an increase in the price of the share, i.e. capital appreciation, and dividend income per share, the price would depend on the capital appreciation one expects. If the share has regularly appreciated by 30% every year, a low dividend yield would be acceptable.

Illustration

The shares of Divya Jeans Ltd. which has a market value of Rs. 40 has appreciated during the last three years by an average percentage of 25. If an investor is aiming at a yield of 30 per cent, a dividend of 5 per cent would be adequate. In such a scenario if Divya Jeans has paid a dividend of 15%, its market value on the basis of dividend per share would be(assuming 15% dividend on the face value = 5% on the market value) as follows:

$$\frac{\text{Rs. 1.50 (dividend)}}{\text{Rs. 5 (return re-}} \times 100 = \text{Rs. 30}$$

On this basis the shares of Divya Jeans is overpriced.

Conversely, if a share does not appreciate by more than 5% and a 30% return is required, a high dividend yield would be expected.

If the shares of PDP have been appreciating at 7% per annum and the company declares a dividend of 30% or Rs. 3 per share the real value of the share would be (30% dividend will be construed as a yield of 23%):

$$\frac{\text{Rs. 3 (dividend per share)}}{\text{Rs. 23 (return required)}} \times 100 = \text{Rs. 13}$$

It must be noted that this method of valuation is so ridden with assumptions (appreciation every year and expected return) that it is rarely used.

Dividend Payout Ratio

The dividend payout ratio measures the quantum or amount of dividend paid out of earning. This ratio enables an investor to determine how much of the annual earnings is paid out as dividend to shareholders and how much is ploughed back into the company for its long-term growth. This is an important ratio when assessing a company's prospects because if all its income is distributed there would be no internal generation of capital available to finance expansion and to nullify the ravages of inflation and to achieve these the company would have to borrow.

This ratio is calculated by dividing the dividend by net income after tax:

$$\text{Dividend Payout Ratio} = \frac{\text{Dividend}}{\text{Net income after tax}}$$

Normally, young, aggressive growth companies have low dividend payout ratios as they plough back their profits for growth. Mature companies, on the other hand, have high payouts. This is of concern as they may not be retaining capital to

Illustration

Excel Railings Ltd.'s earnings after tax in the last financial year was Rs. 68 lakh. Of this, it paid a dividend of Rs. 28 lakh. Its dividend payout ratio would be 28/68 = 0.412.

The company distributed 41.2% of its net income as dividends, retaining 58.8% in the business for its growth.

renew assets or grow. Investors must also ensure that the dividend is being paid out of current income and not out of retained earnings because that tantamounts to eating into the funding set aside for growth, expansion and replacement of assets.

Summary

It is important to remember that earnings ratios are not indicators of profitability. They advise an investor on the earnings made per share, the dividend policy of a company, and the extent of income ploughed back into the company for its expansion, growth and replacement of assets.

It is critical that investors examine these ratios, especially the earnings per share and the dividend payout. The earnings per share would help one determine whether the market price of a share is reasonable. If the dividend payout ratios are very high investors must be concerned as it can indicate that the management of the company is not particularly committed to its long-term growth and prospects.

Profitability

The profitability of a company is of prime importance for an investor. Unless a company is profitable, it cannot grow; it cannot pay dividends; its value will not increase and it cannot survive in the long run.

Profitability ratios assist an investor in determining how well a particular company is doing *vis-a-vis* other companies within the same industry, and with reference to its own performance in earlier years. With the help of these ratios, an investor can evaluate the management's effectiveness on the basis of the returns generated on sales and investments.

While calculating and evaluating a company's profitability, an investor must bear the following in mind:

- As far as possible ratios must be calculated on average assets and liabilities and not on the assets or liabilities on a particular date. There can be large variations in these figures during the year which can distort results quite materially. Companies have also been known to window dress their balance sheets by either reducing or increasing assets or liabilities. Moreover, since profits are earned not on a particular date but over a year, ratios calculated on average assets and liabilities would portray a truer indication of the results achieved by a company.
- The investor should bear in mind the rate of inflation and the cost of capital and borrowings. When evaluating a profitability ratio, an investor should consider whether a better return would have been received elsewhere. And whether the return has kept pace with the rate of inflation.
- Finally, ratios should be considered as an indication or as a suggestion of future development.

Return on Total Assets

The first ratio one should check is the return on total assets. This is an extremely important indicator as it would help the investor determine:

- Whether the company has earned a reasonable return on its sales.
- Whether the company's assets have been effectively and efficiently used, and

- Whether the cost of the company's borrowings are too high.

This ratio should be used to compare the performance of a company with other companies within the same industry, and with previous years. It could also be used to project the performance of future years:

$$\text{ROA} = \frac{\text{Net income after tax}}{\text{Average total asset}}$$

Illustration

Nair Limited is a company engaged in the manufacture of refrigerators and washing machines.

	Year-1	Year-2	Year-3
	Rs. (lakh)	*Rs. (lakh)*	*Rs. (lakh)*
Net income after tax	300	400	600
Total assets	5,000	7,000	11,000

The return on total assets are as follows:

Year-2 $$\frac{400}{0.5 \times (5{,}000 + 7{,}000)} = 6.67\%$$

Year-3 $$\frac{600}{0.5 \times (7{,}000 - 11{,}000)} = 6.67\%$$

Although net income has improved by 50%, the company's profitability has not improved since its average assets have also increased by 50%.

Return on Equity

Another important measure of profitability is the return on equity, or ROE as it is often termed. The purpose of this ratio is to determine whether the return earned is as good as other alternatives available. This return is calculated by expressing income, i.e. the net profit after tax, as a percentage of share holders' equity. It is to be noted that the income figure should not include extraordinary, unusual or non recurring items as that would distort the results arrived at. In addition, the net income on which this ratio is calculated should exclude dividends on preference shares. Shareholders' equity is the stake ordinary shareholders have in a company and includes, reserves and retained earnings.

$$\text{ROE} = \frac{\text{Net income after tax — Dividend on preference shares}}{\text{Average shareholders' equity}}$$

Illustration

The published results of Homedale Limited included the following:

	Year-1	Year-2	Year-3
	Rs. (lakh)	*Rs. (lakh)*	*Rs. (lakh)*
Income before tax		1,100	1,700
Extraordinary Items		300	---
		1,400	1,700
Taxation		400	500
Income after taxation		1,000	1,200
Shareholders' equity	10,000	11,000	12,200

Note: The tax applicable to the extraordinary profit is Rs. 200 lakh.

The Return on Equity in the two years would be:

$$\text{Year-2} \quad \frac{1{,}000-(300-200)}{0.5 \times (10{,}000 + 11{,}000)} = 8.57\%$$

$$\text{Year-3} \quad \frac{1{,}200}{0.5 \times (11{,}000 + 12{,}200)} = 10.34\%$$

The ROE has improved in Year-3. The investor would however need to determine whether this is the best return that he could have got, i.e. could he have earned more if he had invested his money elsewhere.

It must be remembered that if there are other investments that earn a higher return with lower risks then the profitability is low. The ROE should be compared with other alternatives taking into account the risks of the investment. The normal rule is: the higher the return, the higher the risk.

Pre-interest Return on Assets

It is often said that the pre-interest return on assets is a purer measure of profitability since it is difficult to compare the post-tax performance of companies on account of interest and taxation. This is because the interest paid will vary from company to company and will depend on its borrowings. Similarly, the tax liability of companies differs and depends on the manner in which it has planned its tax. This ratio therefore suggests that the return should be based on operating income and is arrived at by dividing earnings before interest and tax by the average total assets:

$$\text{Pre-interest return on assets} = \frac{\text{Earning before interest and tax}}{\text{Average total assets}}$$

Illustration

Rampole Menon Ltd.

	Year-1 *Rs. (lakh)*	Year-2 *Rs. (lakh)*
Earnings before interest & tax	250	300
Total assets	1,000	1,400

Pre-interest return on assets would be:

$$\frac{300}{0.5 \times (1000 + 1400)} \times 100 = 12.1.2\%$$

An investor must compare the return earned by a company with that of other companies, preferably in the same industry, to determine whether the return earned is high or low.

Pre-interest After Tax Return of Assets

The purpose of calculating this ratio is to determine the management's performance in deploying assets effectively without financing. Tax is included in the calculation as it is deducted before arriving at the profits. Interest, however, is not considered as it will vary from company to company and is a payment for capital or funds. The ratio is arrived at by expressing net return after tax but exclusive of interest as a percentage of average total assets:

Pre-interest after tax return on assets =

$$\frac{\text{Net income after tax + Interest expense net of income tax saving}}{\text{Average total assets}}$$

Illustration

An extract of the financials of Bhagwan Ltd. is as follows:

	Year-1	Year-2	Year-3
	Rs. (crore)	*Rs. (crore)*	*Rs. (crore)*
Earnings before Interest & tax		800	1,200
Interest expense		200	400
Pretax income		600	800
Tax at 50%		300	400
Net income after tax		300	400
Total assets	7,000	9,000	11,000

Contd . . .

Pre-interest after tax return on tax is as follows:

Year-2 $$\frac{600 + 200 \times \frac{50}{100}}{0.5\,(7000 + 9000)} = 8.75\ \%$$

Year-3 $$\frac{800 + 400 \times \frac{50}{100}}{0.5\,(9000 + 11000)} = 10.00\ \%$$

In Year-2, Bhagwan Ltd. earned a return on assets prior to the cost of financing of 8.75%. This improved to 10.00 % in Year-3, suggesting that the assets had been used more effectively in the latter year. However while comparing other companies one should compare the return and determine whether the return is adequate (considering the size and the nature of the company.)

Return on Total Invested Capital

The ratio used for determining whether the capital available to a company has been efficiently used is the return on total invested capital. By using this ratio, an investor can check whether he could have earned more elsewhere. It therefore gives him an opportunity to compare returns from alternative companies. Invested capital in this ratio includes all liabilities that have a cost associated with them, such as debentures, share capital and loans. The ratio is arrived at by dividing a company's earnings before interest and tax by average total invested capital:

$$\text{Return on total invested capital} = \frac{\text{Earnings before interest \& tax}}{\text{Average total invested capital}}$$

Illustration

Bombay Pistons Ltd's earnings before interest and tax in the current year was Rs. 18.50 crore. Its total invested capital in the current year and the previous year was as follows:

	Previous Year	Current Year
	Rs. (crore)	*Rs. (crore)*
Term Loan	150	120
Debentures	500	500
Shareholders' funds	80	85
	---------	--------
Total invested capital	730	705
	--------	-------

The return on total invested capital is:

$$\frac{18.50}{0.5 \times (730 + 705)} \times 100 = 2.58$$

An investor must check whether the return on capital is higher than the prevailing rate of interest and the weighted average cost of borrowings. If the rate of interest is higher then the return on the capital should be considered inadequate.

Summary

The profitability ratios are arguably the most important of all ratios for an investor as they indicate whether an enterprise is viable, and better or worse than other similar ones. These ratios however should not be seen in isolation. One should remember that a lower ratio is not necessarily bad. In order to increase sales and profits companies may sell goods at lower prices in volume driven businesses. Like all ratios, these ratios are indicators and they should be considered as such.

Liquidity

Liquidity is one of the cornerstones of any investment. It is important that investments be liquid so that they can be converted to cash easily to meet obligations. Similarly, it is important for a company to be liquid in order for it to meet its maturing financial obligations and to have enough funds to meet its operational requirements. If a company is unable to do so, it may be forced to sell its more important assets at a loss and, in extreme cases, be forced into liquidation. After the securities scam in 1992, many mutual funds were forced to sell their blue chip shares to generate liquidity as they were not able to sell their large holdings of securities of public sector undertakings (PSUs). In the first quarter of 2000 when the values of Information Technology shares plummeted there was fear that prices would fall further as mutual funds sold shares to meet redemptions of their units. When the UTI went through its troubles, Mr. Damodaran after taking charge orchestrated a sale of the more marketable securities to book profits and to be liquid to meet redemption demands.

Current Ratio

The current ratio is the most commonly used ratio to measure liquidity. Its purpose is to check whether a company's current assets are enough to meet its immediate liabilities, i.e. those that mature within one year. The ratio is arrived at by dividing current assets by current liabilities:

$$\text{Current ratio} = \frac{\text{Current assets}}{\text{Current liabilities}}$$

> ***Illustration***
>
> At 31 March, Spear Canisters Ltd's current assets were Rs. 400 crore whereas its current liabilities were Rs. 125 crore. Its current ratio is, therefore, 16:5 or 3.2. In short, Spear Canisters Ltd. can easily meet its current liabilities. It can do so by selling a mere 31.25% of its current assets.

Normally, the current ratio is around 1 or even a little below 1. This in itself is not bad. Today, all companies are aware of the cost of capital, the opportunity cost of tying up capital unproductively, and just in time (JIT) inventory control. Consequently, there is an effort to keep current assets low, be it stock levels, debtors or cash. Thus, often the current ratio is well below 1. This does not necessarily mean that the company is illiquid, it could merely be using its assets effectively.

Quick or Acid Test

The acid test is a favourite of investors and creditors. This ratio is used to check whether a company has enough cash or cash equivalents to meet its current obligations or liabilities. The underlying logic being that there usually is no conversion cost when cash or cash equivalents are used to pay debts. Other assets such as inventories (stocks) may realise less than book value if sold at a distress. In other words, company could lose when converting these to cash in an emergency.

This ratio is arrived at by dividing cash, marketable investments and debtors by current liabilities. It is to be noted that investments, though strictly not a current asset, is used in calculating this ratio. This is because they are easily realisable:

$$\text{Quick ratio} = \frac{\text{Cash and cash equivalents}}{\text{Current liabilities}}$$

Illustration

An extract of Nivya Ltd's financial statement at 31 March was as follows:

	Rs (lakh)
Cash at Bank	150
Debtors	1850
Stocks	3100
Investments	500

Current Assets	5600

Current liabilities	4000

The quick ratio will be:

$$\frac{150+1850+500}{4000} = 0.625$$

The company cannot pay off its entire current liabilities with cash or cash equivalents. It should be remembered that stocks have not been considered in calculating this ratio as it is not a cash equivalent and, as explained above, if one wishes to sell these in a hurry there is likely to be a loss arising out of dumping of goods.

Net Current Assets

Net current assets or net working investments is arrived at by deducting current liabilities from current working assets (trade assets). This is clearly not a ratio. Its usefulness lies in quickly ascertaining whether a company has adequate current assets to meet its current liabilities. Net current assets is really the working capital of a company. Consequently, several derivatives can be calculated from this figure, such as its relationship to sales, income and even to capital.

Net current assets can also be used as a base to determine the quantum of working capital required to support a certain level of sales. A ratio of 20% could suggest that if sales were to increase by 20%, net current assets would also need to increase proportionately. In this context, it is better to have a low ratio as the increase in working capital needed will be less. The company can therefore grow quite rapidly.

In the example of Samudra Fisheries, net current assets were Rs. 450 lakh and sales Rs. 2000 lakh. Its net current assets to sales would be:

$$\frac{0.5 \times (400+450)}{2{,}000} \times 100 = 21.25\ \%$$

Illustration

In its latest financial year, Samudra Fisheries had a sales turnover of Rs. 2,000 lakh. Its net current assets were:

	Previous Year *(Rs. lakh)*	Latest Year *(Rs. lakh)*
Current Assets		
Debtors	280	310
Stocks	320	390
Total current assets	600	700
Current Liabilities		
Creditors	190	220
Accrued expenses	3	5
Tax payable	7	25
Total current liabilities	200	250
Net current assets	400	450

Samudra Fisheries thus had net current assets of Rs. 450 lakh. This means it had Rs. 450 lakh left after meeting its current obligations.

This means that working capital should increase by 21.25% to support every increase in sales. Thus, if sales were to increase by Rs. 1 crore, working capital would need to necessarily increase by Rs. 21.25 lakh.

Net Trade Cycle

It is important to determine the time a company takes to realise its sales proceeds after paying for the purchase of its raw materials. This is a very useful tool for determining a company's liquidity and is computed by adding the debtors turnover in days to the stock turnover in days, and deducting from it the creditors turnover in days.

$$\text{Debtors turnover} = \frac{\text{Average debtors}}{\text{Sales}} \times 365$$

$$\text{Stock turnover} = \frac{\text{Average stocks}}{\text{Sales}} \times 365$$

$$\text{Creditors turnover} = \frac{\text{Average creditors}}{\text{Sales}} \times 365$$

$$\text{Net trade cycle} = \text{Debtors turnover} - \text{Stock turnover} - \text{Creditors turnover}$$

If this ratio improves, it indicates an improvement in the management of net current working assets. Of course, it can also indicate that the company is experiencing difficulty in paying its creditors. Thus one must go beyond the figures to determine the reasons for a change in the net trade cycle. It must be remembered that the longer the cycle, the greater the need for financing. The net trade cycle should therefore be brought down as much as possible. This can be achieved by reducing debtors and stock levels.

Illustrations

Vindhya Bearings Ltd's financials included the following figures:

	Previous Year *Rs. (crore)*	Latest Year *Rs. (crore)*
Sales	200	280
Cost of goods sold	160	224
Debtors	24	44
Stocks	36	
	48	

The net trade cycle is:

		Days
Debtor turnover	$\frac{0.5 \times (24+44)}{280} \times 365 =$	44
Stock turnover	$\frac{0.5 \times (36+48)}{224} \times 365 =$	68
Less:		
Creditor turnover	$\frac{0.5 \times (16+32)}{224} \times 365 =$	(39)
Net trade cycle (days)	=	73

Investors should apart from checking whether there is an improvement in the cycle, check the individual components. An increase in creditors turnover could also suggest that the company has difficulty in making payments. A fall in debtors could suggest a fall in credit sales or improved debt collection. The reason must be looked into.

Defensive Interval

This ratio indicates the number of days a company can remain in business without any additional financing or sales. It can be likened to a worker on strike. How many days can he survive on the assets that he has before he becomes bankrupt?

The defensive interval ratio is calculated by dividing a company's average daily cash operating expenses by its most liquid assets. It is important to note that only the most liquid of assets are used in calculating this ratio, such as cash and cash equivalents. Debtors and stocks are not to be considered as they are not cash equivalents.

$$\text{Defensive ratio} = \frac{\text{Average daily cash operating expense}}{\text{Most liquid assets}}$$

Illustration

The cash and cash equivalents of General Balls Ltd. a company whose annual operating expenses were Rs. 730 crore were as follows:

	Rs. (crore)
Cash	35
Marketable securities	145
	Rs. 180

Its daily operating expenses would be $\frac{730}{365}$ = Rs. 2 crore

Its defensive interval would be $\frac{180}{2}$ = 90 days

This means that General Balls Ltd. can remain in existence for 90 days without any sales or financing.

Current Liability Coverage

The current liability coverage ratio enables investors to examine the relationship between cash inflows from operations and current liabilities, and to determine whether the company can meet its currently maturing obligations from internally generated funds. At times of creative accounting and cash crunches this is an extremely important ratio:

$$\text{Current liability coverage} = \frac{\text{Cash inflow from operations}}{\text{Average current liabilities}}$$

> ***Illustration***
>
> In its latest year ended 31 March, Bharat Bolts Ltd. earned a net income before tax but after depreciation of Rs. 750 lakh. Depreciation was Rs. 25 lakh. Current liabilities on previous 31 March and current 31 March were Rs. 1,450 lakh and Rs. 2,350 lakh respectively.
>
> The current liability coverage is:
>
> $$\frac{750+25}{0.5\ (1450+2350)} = 0.41$$
>
> In other words, cash flow from operations was only 41 % of current liabilities. If current liabilities were to be paid out of internally generated funds it would take 2.44 years.

Summary

Liquidity is becoming increasingly important for companies and this factor alone has resulted in companies becoming sick — an inadequacy of funds to finance operations. It is crucial that investors examine the liquidity of a company, and whether it is improving or deteriorating.

As companies begin to have financial difficulties, they begin to postpone and delay paying their bills. Current liabilities begin to build up. As current liabilities build up, suppliers become more and more reluctant to sell goods. This first affects production, then sales and has a snowballing effect. Therefore if the liquidity ratios of a company are deteriorating, an investor should be concerned.

However, negative liquidity ratios need not necessarily be bad. Many strong companies keep low current assets and are able to get long credit from suppliers, especially those that operate with extremely low margins.

Historically, companies exhibit excellent liquidity ratios before a crash. This is because fixed assets and stocks are sold and gets converted into cash. Current liabilities decrease as creditors are paid off. So good liquidity is also not always wonderful.

An investor should always check the quality of a company's current assets. It should also be ascertained whether they are at current realisable value. Moreover, current assets should not include deferred revenue expenditure like advertising costs as they do not have any encashable value. Finally, it must be remembered that balance sheets can be window dressed. Therefore, the figures should be properly scrutinised.

The optimal liquidity required varies from company to company and from industry to industry. It depends both on market conditions and the prominence of a company. While viewing liquidity ratios, the investor must check whether a company is adequately liquid and whether its liquidity position has deteriorated or improved. If it has deteriorated and there does not seem a likelihood of it, improving in the imminent future, one should consider selling the company's shares.

Leverage

Leverage indicates the extent to which a company is dependent on borrowed funds to finance its business. These borrowings would be in the form of debentures, term loans, short term loans and bank overdrafts.

In highly leveraged firms, the owners' funds are minimal and the owners are able to control the business with a fairly low stake. The main risks are borne by the lenders. In good times these companies make large profits, especially if they are in high margin businesses. However, the reverse occurs in times of recession. Interest costs are exorbitant and the large profits made in boom times turn into large losses.

The effect on profits is illustrated in Table 9.2. Company A is a highly leveraged, Company B's borrowed funds amount to 20% of its total funds, and Company C is a cash rich company and does not borrow at all. In a good year the return Company A makes is a stupendous 170% before tax, whereas Company C makes a comparatively modest 50%. It must be noted that so long as the return or the earnings rate exceeds the cost of borrowings, a highly leveraged company will make impressive profits. As this rate decreases profits will fall. In a reasonable year, too, the profits of highly leveraged companies would be more than companies that do not borrow. In the example in Table II, it would be noticed that the return before tax of Company A is twice that of Company C.

Table 9.2

	Company A Rs. (lakh)	Company B Rs. (lakh)	Company C Rs. (lakh)
Share Capital	40	160	200
Borrowed Funds	160	40	----
	200	200	200
Good Year			
Earnings before Interest and tax	100	100	100
Interest @ 20% p.a.	32	8	-----
Income before tax	68	92	100
Tax @ 50% p.a.	34	46	50
Income after tax	34	46	50
Return to ordinary shareholders:			
Before tax (%)	170.00	57.50	50.00
After tax (%)	85.00	28.75	25.00
Reasonable Year			
Earnings before Interest and tax	60	60	60
Interest @ 20% p.a.	32	8	-----
Income before tax	28	52	60
Tax at 50%	14	26	30
Income after tax	14	26	30
Return to Ordinary Shareholders:			
Before tax (%)	70.00	32.50	30.00
After tax (%)	30.00	16.25	15.00

Contd . . .

	Company A Rs. (lakh)	Company B Rs. (lakh)	Company C Rs. (lakh)
Bad Year			
Earning before Interest and tax	24	24	24
Interest @ 20% p.a.	32	8	-----
Income before tax	(8)	16	24
Tax @ 50%	-----	8	12
Income after tax	(8)	8	12
Return to Ordinary Shareholders:			
Before tax(%)		10	12
After tax (%)		5	6

The tide turns in years of depression or recession as borrowings have to be serviced. At such times, the cost of borrowings often exceed the profits made and results in losses and the company that makes the highest profits is the one that has no borrowings.

One can safely conclude, therefore, that though companies with very little or no borrowings are safer and can be depended upon for some returns both in good years and bad, highly leveraged companies are risky and earnings can be negative in bad years. Conversely, in good years the results of highly leveraged companies can be very good indeed.

Liabilities to Assets Ratio

This ratio indicates the total borrowings used to finance the company, and the extent to which these external liabilities finances the assets of a company. Liabilities in this context include both current and long term liabilities. Assets include all assets excluding intangibles, such as deferred revenue expenditure (preliminary expenses, goodwill, deferred advertising expenditure and the like). The ratio is calculated by dividing total liabilities by the total assets:

$$\text{Liabilities to assets ratio} = \frac{\text{Total liabilities}}{\text{Total assets}}$$

Illustration

The Balance Sheet of SWW Ltd at 31 March is detailed below:

	Rs. (lakh)
Sources of Funds	
Shareholders' Funds	100
Debentures	50
Current Liabilities	200

	350

Application of Funds	
Fixed Assets	80
Investments	40
Preliminary expenses	10
Current Assets	220

	350

The liabilities to assets ratio would be:

$$\frac{50 + 200}{350 - 10} = 0.74$$

This means that 74% of the assets of the company were financed by liabilities. Conversely, it can also be said that assets sold at even 74% of their book value would meet and extinguish the company's liability commitments.

An investor would be wise to examine also a company's contingent liabilities, such as guarantees, legal suits, and the like.

Should these be significant and likely to crystallise, the ratio would change dramatically.

Debt to Assets Ratio

The debt to assets ratio is a more specific ratio. It determines the extent debt or borrowed funds are covered by assets and measures how much assets can depreciate in value and still meet the debt commitments. Debts are defined as borrowed funds and would include bank overdrafts. Assets exclude intangibles, such as goodwill and deferred assets. The ratio is calculated by dividing debt by total tangible assets:

$$\text{Debt to Assets ratio} = \frac{\text{Total debt}}{\text{Total tangible assets}}$$

Illustration

An extract of the financial statements of Pushpa Refrigerators Ltd. is detailed below:

	Rs. (lakh)
Term Loan	200
14% Debentures	500
Bank overdraft	50

	750

Total assets	1200
Goodwill	100

The Debt to Assets ratio would be:

$$\frac{750}{1200 - 100} = 0.68$$

Even if assets were to reduce by as much as 32%, the company would still be able to meet its commitments.

Debt to Net Worth Ratio

The debt to net worth ratio shows the extent funds are sourced from external sources and hence the extent a company is dependent on borrowings to finance its business. It is arrived at by dividing a company's debt by its net worth. Net worth is defined as shareholders' equity, less intangible assets:

$$\text{Debt to net worth} = \frac{\text{Debt}}{\text{Net worth}}$$

Illustration

Nikhila Ltd's debt on 31 March was Rs. 385 lakh. The shareholders' equity was Rs. 105 lakh. There were no intangible assets.

The debt to net worth ratio was:

$$\frac{385}{105} = 3.67$$

In other words, borrowed funds were 3.67 times the shareholders' equity. For every Re. 1 invested by shareholders, borrowings were Rs. 3.67. This shows the company is highly geared.

Liabilities to Net Worth

The liabilities to net worth is a larger measure than the debt to net worth ratio and attempts to determine how dependent a company is on liabilities to fund its business. It is calculated by dividing the total liabilities of a company by its net worth. Net worth is arrived at after deducting intangible assets:

$$\text{Liabilities to net worth ratio} = \frac{\text{Total liabilities}}{\text{Net worth}}$$

Illustration

The Balance Sheet of Ravi Hawaii Ltd. is as follows:

	Rs. (lakh)
Shareholder's equity	158
Debentures	150
Term loans	40
Current Liabilities	40

	388

Tangible Assets	378
Intangibles	10

	388

The liability to net worth ratio would be:

$$\frac{230}{158 - 10} = 1.55$$

The company's liabilities are thus 1.55 times its net worth. Alternatively, liabilities finance 60.85% of the assets (230/230+(158–10). This is an extremely useful ratio when one is determining how well shareholders would be compensated should the company go into liquidation.

Incremental Gearing

The incremental gearing ratio attempts to determine the additional borrowings required to finance growth. To an extent this ratio is similar to the net working investments ratio. The ratio is calculated by dividing the net increase in debt by the increase in net income after tax but before dividend:

$$\text{Incremental gearing} = \frac{\text{Net increase in debt}}{\text{Increase in net income after tax but before dividend}}$$

Illustration

The financials of Raman Tea Ltd. were as follows:

	Previous Year	Latest Year
	Rs. 00s	*Rs. 00s*
Net income before tax	300	400
Taxation	50	75
	--------	-------
	250	325
	--------	-------
Borrowings	400	480

The incremental gearing is: $\dfrac{0.5 \times (480 - 400)}{75} = 75$

For every Re. 1 used to finance growth, net income would increase by Rs. 75. That is a very high dependence.

Other Ratios

There are several other gearing ratios but these are seldom used. For instance, the long-term debt ratio determines how important borrowings are to total long-term liabilities and shareholders' equity. Another ratio is the liability to equity issue. Liabilities in this calculation includes total liabilities as well as shareholders' equity.

Summary

The gearing ratios highlight the dependence a company has on external funds and the extent to which liabilities finance the company. These ratios are extremely important for investors to consider while evaluating a company.

Debt Service Capacity

Debt is a source of finance which has become increasingly popular in recent years. Fifteen years ago few companies issued or offered convertible and non convertible debentures. Now, there are more debentures, of one kind or another being offered than equity. In this scenario, the investor must ascertain whether a company can service its debt through internally generated funds. Can it meet the principal and interest payments out of its profits? This of course is based on the assumption that the company is a profitable going concern and that debt will not be repaid through additional borrowings or rights and public issues of shares.

Debt Coverage

This ratio is used to determine the time it would take a company to repay its short and long term debt from its income or internally generated funds. This is relevant if the debt is not to be extinguished through the sale of assets, or by the issue of fresh capital or debt.

For calculating this ratio, internally generated funds mean income after tax plus non-cash expenses such as depreciation, and non operating income and expenses. Debt would comprise of bank overdrafts, term loans and debentures. The ratio is calculated by dividing a company's internally generated funds by its average debt:

$$\text{Debt coverage ratio} = \frac{\text{Internally generated funds}}{\text{Average debt}}$$

Illustration

An extract of the financials of Pear Ltd. included the following:

	Previous Year *Rs. (crore)*	Latest Year *Rs. (crore)*
Net income before tax and depreciation		500
Depreciation		100

Net profit before tax		400
Tax		160

Net profit after tax		240

Bank overdraft	100	150
Debentures	400	380
Term loan	100	90
	-------	-------
	600	520
	-------	-------

Debt coverage ratio would be:

$$\frac{240+100}{0.5 \times (600+520)} = 0.60$$

This means that it would take Pear Ltd. 1.7 years to repay borrowers from its profits.

Liability Coverage

Liability coverage ratio is an extension of the debt coverage ratio. It is used to check whether a company can repay all liabilities through internal generation. This ratio is calculated by dividing the internally generated funds of a company by its average total liabilities:

$$\text{Liability coverage ratio} = \frac{\text{Internally generated funds}}{\text{Average total liabilities}}$$

Illustration

In its latest year ended 31 March, Tongues and Tongs Ltd. generated Rs. 500 lakh internally. Its total liabilities at the end of the previous year and the latest year were Rs. 3,500 lakh and Rs. 4,500 lakh, respectively.

$$\text{The liability coverage ratio} = \frac{500}{0.5 \times (3500+4500)} = 0.25$$

This means that internally generated funds were only 25 percent of the company's total average liabilities. At this level, the entire debt can be paid off in 4 years.

It is also possible to calculate this ratio using the liabilities figure at the date of the balance sheet, the argument being that what has to be considered is the time it would take to repay the total liabilities at a particular time.

Interest Cover

An important factor that investors must ascertain is whether a company's profits are adequate to meet its interest dues. If not, the interest will have to be paid from either from the company's reserves, additional borrowings, or from a fresh issue of capital and these are a sure sign of financial weakness.

The interest cover ratio is calculated by dividing a company's earnings before interest and tax by its interest expense. The ratio must always be in excess of 1 — and the higher it is the better. If it is below 1, even a marginal fall in profit would force the company to pay interest out of its retained earnings or capital.

$$\text{Interest cover ratio} = \frac{\text{Earnings before interest and tax}}{\text{Interest expense}}$$

Illustration

Bombay Green Ltd. earned Rs. 450 crore before interest and tax in its latest financial year. Its interest expense was Rs. 200 crore.

$$\text{Interest cover ratio} = \frac{450}{200} = 2.25$$

The company's earnings before interest are more than double its interest expense. A comfortable situation.

Fixed Charge Cover

The eighties witnessed the birth and the development of several financing and leasing companies in India. These companies offer the opportunity of leasing equipment as opposed to purchasing it. One benefit of leasing is that the rentals paid are entirely tax deductible. Secondly, funds do not need to be deployed for the purchase of assets.

This is known as "off balance sheet financing", i.e. neither the real cost of the asset nor its liability is reflected in the balance sheet. The fixed charge cover considers off balance sheet obligations, such as rental expenses, and checks whether a company earns enough income to meet its interest and rental commitments:

$$\text{Fixed charge cover} = \frac{\text{Earnings before interest and taxes + Rental expense}}{\text{Interest and rental expense}}$$

Illustration

Ram Oil Soaps Ltd's income statement included the following figures:

	Rs. (crore)
Rental expense	400
Earnings before interest and tax	750
Interest	200
Earnings before tax	550
Tax @ 40	220
Profit after tax	330

$$\text{Fixed charge cover} = \frac{750 + 400}{200 + 400} = 1.91$$

At times it is argued that the dividend payable on preferred shares should also be accounted for in calculating this ratio as it is a fixed charge that has to be paid. In that case, the fixed charge cover is calculated in two stages. In the first stage, the fixed charge cover is calculated as explained above, and then the preferred dividends paid are taken into account:

$$\frac{\text{Net Income} + (1 - \text{Tax rate})\ (\text{Interest and rental expenses})}{(1 - \text{Tax rate})\ (\text{Interest and rental expense}) + \text{Preferred dividends}}$$

This is a better ratio than the interest cover ratio as it considers all the fixed expenses that a company has and examines whether its earnings are sufficient to meet these.

Cash Flow Surplus

The cash flow surplus ratio is based on the going concern concept and assumes that companies will normally grow and will therefore incur capital expenditure and that there would be an increase in its net working capital. As such, a company's ability to pay its debt should be determined only after providing for increases in its capital expenditure and net working capital. Cash flow is net income plus non cash charges, i.e. depreciation, etc. less capital expenditure and increases in net working investments. The ratio is calculated by dividing the cash flow surplus by the total debt.

$$\text{Cash flow surplus} = \frac{\text{Cash flow surplus}}{\text{Total average debt}}$$

Illustration

In its latest financial year, the average debt of Culture Ltd. was Rs. 400 crore. Its internally generated funds were Rs. 40 crore. Its net working investments had increased by Rs. 10 crore and the company had incurred capital expenditure of Rs. 20 crore.

$$\text{Cash flow surplus} = \frac{40 - 10 - 20}{400} = 0.025$$

It would take the company 40 years to repay its debts by utilizing its cash flow surplus.

This ratio is often negative. This is because when a company grows rapidly its purchases assets of a capital nature and its net working investments also increase and this increase is usually more than its internally generated funds. This is usually funded by loans or short-term bank facilities.

Summary

Investors must always consider debt service ratios as these help to determine whether the company under consideration has the capacity to service its debts and repay its liabilities. This becomes all the more critical at times of high inflation and recession when the inability to service debt can plunge a company into bankruptcy.

Asset Management / Efficiency

It is by the efficient management of assets that companies make profits. Accordingly, investors must determine whether the assets a company has are adequate to meet its needs and whether the returns are reasonable. It must be remembered that assets are acquired either from capital or from borrowings. If there are more assets than is necessary, the company is locking up funds it could have used more profitably or, conversely, is paying interest needlessly. If the assets are less than required, the company's operations would not be using its resources as productively and effectively as possible.

Asset management ratios allow investors to determine whether a company has adequate assets and is utilizing them efficiently.

It is assumed that sales volumes are affected by the utilization of assets. Asset ratios are used to assess trends and to determine how well assets have been utilized. Comparisons can be made between one year and the next, between one company and another in the same industry, and in other industries. These ratios also help enormously in making forecasts and budgets.

It must be remembered, however, that like other ratios asset management ratios too are pointers. A high asset turnover does not necessarily suggest great efficiency or a high return on investments, it may be so because a company does not maintain adequate assets and this can affect its performance in the long run. Investors should therefore always look beyond the indications. It is important to bear in mind that a deterioration in asset ratios is a sign of decline and should be heeded.

Stock utilization

The stock utilization ratios measure how efficiently a company's stocks are used. With the cost of borrowings being high, managers are constantly alert to the need to keep stocks low. In these days of the just-in-time principle, these ratios are always carefully scrutinized and evaluated.

Stock utilization can be measured by two ratios:

Stock turnover ratio

This ratio indicates the number of times stocks (inventory) are turned over in a year and is calculated by dividing the cost of goods sold in a year by the average stocks held in a year:

$$\text{Stock turnover ratio} = \frac{\text{Cost of goods sold}}{\text{Average stock}}$$

Stock holding ratio

The stock holding ratio measures the number of days of stocks (in relation to sales) held by a company. With companies attempting to keep as little stock as possible, this is an important efficiency indicator. It is calculated by expressing the stock held in terms of the days of cost of goods sold:

$$\text{Stock holding ratio} = \frac{\text{Average stock}}{\text{Cost of goods sold divided by 365}}$$

Illustration

The average inventory of Nandan Switchgears Ltd. was Rs. 150 crore in the previous year and Rs. 160 crore in its latest financial year. During this period the cost of goods sold was Rs. 1,050 crore and Rs. 1,200 crore, respectively. The ratios are as follows:

Stock turnover ratio:

Previous Year $\frac{1050}{150}$ = 7 times

Latest Year $\frac{1200}{160}$ = 7.5 times

Stock holding ratio:

Previous Year $\frac{150}{1050 \times 365}$ = 52.14 days

Latest Year $\frac{160}{1200 \times 365}$ = 48.67 days

Nandan Switchgears Ltd. has successfully reduced inventory levels by 3.47 days of production and turned over stock 0.5 times more. This is usually good.

Investors should ascertain the reason for the improvement in stocks, i.e. is it because stocks have been dumped on dealers, due to difficulties in procuring stocks, or due to a strike in the manufacturing plants? As companies close down stock levels fall. Purchases are not made and existing stocks are sold. The reasons for the improvement in this ratio must therefore be ascertained. In addition, an investor should try and ascertain whether the existing level of stocks can support the level of sales a company has.

Average Collection Period

Most companies sell to their customers on credit. To finance these sales, they need to either block their own internal funds or resort to bank finance. The cost of finance is therefore usually built into the sale price and companies offer a cash discount to customers who pay in cash either at the time of sale or soon thereafter.

The average collection ratio is calculated by dividing average trade debtors by the average daily sales:

$$\text{Average collection period} = \frac{\text{Average trade debtors}}{\text{Average sales per day}}$$

Illustration

In its latest year, the sales of PDN Ltd. grew by 15%, from Rs. 348 crore to Rs. 400 crore. Its average trade debtors during the previous and current years were Rs. 49 crore and Rs. 59 crore, respectively.

The average collection period was therefore:

Previous Year $\quad \dfrac{49}{348 \times 365} = 51 \text{ days}$

Current Year $\quad \dfrac{59}{400 \times 365} = 54 \text{ days}$

The period of credit increased from the previous year. If PDN Ltd's normal credit terms are only 30 days and customers are taking 51 to 54 days to pay, the company is finding difficulty in getting its customers to pay on time, or it may be extending longer periods of credit, or the management may not be controlling credit effectively.

An increasing average collection period ratio is an early warning indicator of large bad debts and financial sickness and by controlling thus one can improve efficiency and reduce borrowings, thereby saving on interest.

A falling ratio is not however always wonderful. Just before companies fold up, they begin collecting on their debts and also sell their goods for cash. The result is a falling average collection period ratio.

Average Payment Period

The average payment period ratio or the creditor ratio indicates the time it takes a company to pay its trade creditors, i.e. the number of days' credit it enjoys. The ratio is calculated by dividing trade creditors by the average daily cost of goods sold:

$$\text{Average payment period} = \frac{\text{Trade creditors}}{\text{Average daily cost of goods sold}}$$

Illustration

True Steel Ltd. is a large company based in Pondicherry. Its financials indicated that its average trade creditors in the previous and latest year were Rs. 29 crore and Rs. 34 crore, respectively. Its cost of goods sold was Rs. 410 crore in the previous year and Rs. 425 crore in the current year.

Its average payment period would be:

Previous Year $\frac{29}{410 \times 365} = 26 \text{ days}$

Current Year $\frac{34}{425 \times 365} = 29 \text{ days}$

In this illustration, the average payment period ratio is low, though it has improved over the previous year. The investor should determine whether:

- The company is availing all the credit that it can.
- The company is having difficulty in procuring credit.
- The company is having difficulty in paying its creditors.

If the company is in a strong and commanding position, it can obtain longer credit terms. This is good since the company can effectively use creditors to finance its working capital and to that extent the cost of finance falls.

Net Working Investments Ratio

Net working investments are those assets that directly affect sales such as trade debtors, stocks and trade creditors. The ratio is calculated by dividing the net working assets by sales.

$$\text{Net working investments ratio} = \frac{\text{Stocks + Debtors – Creditors}}{\text{Sales}}$$

Illustration

In the latest financial year, the average stocks, debtors and creditors of Tamara Ltd. were Rs. 38 crore, Rs. 45 crore and Rs. 30 crore, respectively. Its sales in that year were Rs. 500 crore.

Net working investments ratio =

$$\frac{38 + 45 - 30}{500} = 0.086$$

The company's net working investments were 8.6% of its sales. If this is the optimum level, then for every Rs. 100 lakh of sales, net working investments would need to rise by Rs. 8.6 lakh. This ratio is therefore extremely useful in assessing working capital requirements.

In short, this ratio highlights the working capital requirements of a company and helps an investor determine whether the company's working capital is controlled efficiently.

Total Asset Utilization

The total asset utilization ratio is calculated in order to determine whether a company is generating sales commensurate with its investment in assets. It indicates how efficiently assets are being utilized and is an extremely useful ratio for preparing forecasts. The ratio is calculated by dividing the sales by the average total assets.

$$\text{Total asset utilization} = \frac{\text{Sale}}{\text{Average total assets}}$$

Illustration

Divya Tyres Ltd. was successful in increasing its sales in the latest financial year to Rs. 630 crore from Rs. 495 crore in the previous year. Its average assets grew by 10% to Rs. 90 crore. Its total asset utilization ratios for the two years were:

Previous Year $\frac{495}{82} = 6.03$

Latest Year $\frac{630}{90} = 7.0$

It is clear that the total assets utilization ratio has increased. This means, too, that the assets required to support an increase in sales have decreased, suggesting that assets are possibly being better utilized.

Fixed Asset Utilization

The fixed asset utilization ratio measures how well a company is utilizing its fixed assets. Investors can compare this with the utilization of other companies in the same industry to determine how effectively a company is utilizing its fixed assets. It should be remembered that this ratio needs to calculated on net fixed assets, i.e. cost less accumulated depreciation. It is arrived at by dividing sales by the average net fixed assets.

$$\text{Net fixed asset utilization} = \frac{\text{Sales}}{\text{Net fixed assets}}$$

Illustration

The relevant financials of Nikhila Pistons Ltd. were as follows:

	Year-1 *Rs. (crore)*	Year-2 *Rs. (crore)*	Year-3 *Rs. (crore)*
Sales	540	580	620
Fixed Assets			
Gross	105	130	150
Accumulated Depreciation	60	65	70
	45	65	70

The net fixed asset utilization was:

Year - 2 $\quad \dfrac{580}{(45 + 65) \div 2} = 10.55$

Year - 3 $\quad \dfrac{620}{(65 + 80) \div 2} = 8.55$

Although sales increased by only 8%, fixed assets went up by 31%. This suggests that the company might be expanding and the fruits or the result of this expansion was yet to be reflected in the net fixed asset utilization.

An increasing net fixed asset utilization ratio suggests that sales may have fallen and the efficiency in the handling of net fixed assets deteriorated.

It must be borne in mind that this ratio is not truly reflective of performance as fixed asset costs will differ when comparing companies. A new company with recently acquired fixed assets will show a worse ratio than one that has old assets. In such a scenario, it would be unfair to label the older company inefficient.

Summary

Asset management ratios are calculated to assess the competence and the effective of management by determining how efficiently assets have been managed. It also highlights how effectively credit policy has been administered and whether a company is availing of all the credit it is entitled to, and is offered, by its suppliers. It can also indicate whether a company is encountering difficulties.

Margins

It is not uncommon to read in annual reports that "although sales have increased by 24 percent in the year profits have fallen due to increases in the cost of production causing margins to erode".

Margins indicate the earnings a company makes on its sales, i.e. its mark up on the cost of the items it manufactures or trades in. The higher the mark up, the greater the profit per item sold and *vice versa*. Margins are so important that they determine the success or failure of a business. And the mark up or margin made by the seller is usually based on what he believes the market can bear, or that which he thinks will fuel sales. Usually, low volume businesses are high margin businesses as goods often have to be held for some time. Others, such as supermarkets or for that matter brokers, work at very low margins because volumes are very high.

Margins help to determine the cost structure of a business, i.e. is it high cost or low cost, and whether the business is a high volume low margin business or otherwise. This is important as it will indicate how dependent the company is on margins. If the company operates with low margins a small increase in costs can result in large losses.

The performance between companies within an industry or a group can also be compared with the help of margins. Let us assume that the gross margin earned by Hindustan York is 20 percent whereas the industry average is 18 percent. It can be argued in this instance that Hindustan York is more efficient and that its products command a greater premium.

Management trends can also be assessed by margins. Efficient and strong managements will work to improve margin or, at least maintain them.

Margins help an investor determine whether increases in costs, whether on account of inflation or governmental levies, have been passed onto customers in part or in full. Should there be a strong demand for the company's product, it will pass on the entire cost increase to the customers. On the other hand, if the demand for the company's products is not very high, the company would often bear a part of the cost increase because of the fear that the customer would not purchase the product. A good example of falling margins is the TV industry. As competition is intense and the buyer has a choice between several brands, manufacturers have been bearing a portion of cost increases and, in some instances, have dropped their prices in order to be competitive.

Product mix has an effect on margins. A company may be selling several products — each of them priced differently. Some may be high margin products and others low margin ones. If more high margin products are sold, the margin earned by the company would be high. Conversely, if more low margin products are sold, the average margin earned on sales will reduce. It must be remembered that low margin businesses are not bad. Some of the most successful businesses in the world are low margin ones that operate with very high turnovers and produce an impressive return on capital employed.

Gross Margin

The gross margin is the surplus available to meet the company's expenses. It is calculated by dividing the difference between sales and the cost of goods sold, and expressing it as a percentage of sales:

$$\text{Gross margin} = \frac{\text{Sales} - \text{Cost of goods sold}}{\text{Sales}} \times 100$$

Illustration

The following figures were extracted from the financial statements of Hindustan York Ltd.

	Year-1	Year-2
	Rs. (crore)	*Rs. (crore)*
Sales	400	500
Cost of sales	275	350
	--------	--------
	125	150
	--------	--------
Gross margin (%)	31.25	30.00

Contd . . .

In Year-2 Hindustan York's sales increased by 25% to Rs.500 crore and it's gross profit increased by Rs. 25 crore, or 20%. Both of these, in these difficult times, are positive. However its gross margin fell by 1.25%. This could be due to several reasons, such as:

- Increased competition: the company reduced its margins to boost sales.
- The company took a conscious decision to reduce its margins in order to improve sales.
- A deterioration in the product mix.
- The company was unable to pass on cost increases to its customers.

An investor should not jump to a conclusion on seeing an improvement or a deterioration in the gross margin. He must go beyond the figures and seek the reasons for the change. An increase in the margin may simply be due to an increase in price whereas a fall could be due either as a consequence of a conscious decision to increase sales or company's inability to pass inflationary cost increases on to customers.

Operating Margin

The profitability of a company before the incidence of tax, miscellaneous income and interest costs is indicated by the operating margin. The operating margin can be arrived at by deducting, selling, general and administrative expenses from the gross profit, and expressing it as a percentage of sales:

$$\text{Operating margin} = \frac{\text{Gross profit} - \text{Selling, general \& admin, expenses}}{\text{Sales}} \times 100$$

Illustration

The relevant information in the results of Patel Nair Ltd. was:

	Previous Year *(Rs. lakh)*	Latest Year *(Rs. lakh)*
Sales	3000	4000
Cost of goods sold	2400	3200
	---------	---------
Gross profit	600	800
Selling, general and administration expenses	400	500
	------	------
Operating profit	200	300
	-----	-----
Operating margin (%)	6.33	7.50

There was an improvement in the operating margin by 1.17%. One of the reasons for this could be that operating expenses did not increase as much as the sales. Sales grew by 33% as did the gross profit, whereas operating expenses grew by 25%. This could be one of the reasons though not the only one. In another situation, despite the sales going up the gross margin may decrease and costs increase resulting in a fall in the operating margin. Normally the operating margin should improve with sales since costs do not usually rise at the same rate. In a recession, or at a time of high inflation, the reverse can be true. Costs may increase at a faster rate than sales and gross margins may also fall.

An investor must always examine the operating margin ratio as it indicates the likely reasons for an improvement, or a deterioration, in a company's profitability and one must ascertain the actual causes for this.

Breakeven Margin

Every organisation has certain expenses, like selling, administration and other miscellaneous expenses that it has to bear even if there are no sales. The breakeven margin indicates the number of units that a company must sell to meet these expenses. If a company's breakeven is at 50% of its capacity, it means that the company would be in a no-profit-no-loss position if it produced and sold half its capacity. Any unit sold above this would yield a profit, and *vice versa*.

The breakeven margin ratio is arrived at by dividing expenses including financing costs, by the gross income per unit. Non-recurring or unusual profits must be excluded from the calculation.

$$\text{Breakeven margin} = \frac{\text{Expenses} - \text{financing costs}}{\text{Gross income / Number of units sold}}$$

Illustration

The results of Kumar Wheels Ltd. during the latest year ended 31 March were as follows:

		Rs. (lakh)
Sales		8000
Less:	Costs of sales	6000

	Gross Income	2000
Less:	Expenses	1200

	Operating income	800
Add:	Profit on sale of factory	50

	Earning before interest and tax	850
Less:	Interest charges	150

	Earnings before tax	700

Contd . . .

The total number of units sold were 1000

Breakeven margin $= \dfrac{1200 + 150}{2000 / 1000} = 675$ units

Kumar Wheels Ltd. have to sell, at present costs, 675 units to bear its expenses. If it sells 676 units it would make a profit of Rs. 2. The company would lose Rs. 2 should it sell only 674 units.

Some investors prefer to calculate the breakeven margin by deducting selling costs from the gross profit to arrive at the gross profit per unit. This is done because selling costs are connected with sales and no selling expenses would be incurred if no sales are made. If, in the example of Kumar Wheels Ltd. stated above, selling expenses were 400, the breakeven margin would be calculated as:

$$\frac{1200 - 400 + 150}{2000 - 400 / 1000} = 593.7 \text{ units}$$

This is arguably a purer measure.

The breakeven margin is an important measure as it indicates exactly how many units need to be sold by a company before it can begin to make profit. This is an important management ratio, too, in decision making when alternatives are being considered.

Pre-Financing Margin

The pre-financing margin is the rate of profit earned prior to the costs of financing. The reason for excluding financing costs is that these vary from organisation to organisation. These also vary on account of the method of financing. The pre-financing margin is therefore calculated by dividing earnings before interest and tax by sales, and expressing this as a percentage.

$$\text{Pre-financing margin} = \frac{\text{Earnings before interest and tax}}{\text{Sales}} \times 100$$

Illustration

In the earlier example of Kumar Wheels Ltd. the relevant figures were:

	Rs. (lakh)
Sales	8,000
Earnings before interest and tax	850

$$\text{Pre-financing margin} = \frac{850}{8{,}000} \times 100 = 10.25\ \%$$

It would be more appropriate to calculate the pre-financing margin after excluding non-recurring income or expenses. In that case, the Rs. 50 lakh profit on the sale of a factory should be deducted and the margin would be:

$$\frac{850 - 50}{8{,}000} \times 100 = 10\ \%$$

This is a good measure for comparing the profitability of organizations.

Pre-tax Margin

The pre-tax margin indicates the rate of profit earned on sales after accounting for the cost of financing but before tax. In short, this is calculated on the income before tax and expressed as a percentage of sales.

$$\text{Pre-tax margin} = \frac{\text{Pre-tax income}}{\text{Sales}} \times 100$$

Illustration

Kumar Wheels Ltd

	Rs. (Lakh)
Sales	8,000
Earning before tax	700

Pre-tax margin would be $\frac{700}{8,000} \times 100 = 8.75\ \%$

As mentioned earlier, non-recurring income or expense should not be included in the calculation as it would distort comparisons. If the Rs. 50 lakh of non-recurring income is omitted, the margin would reduce to 8.125% as follows:

$$\frac{700 - 50}{8,000} \times 100 = 8.125\ \%$$

Pre-tax margin is not a fair measure of profitability and comparison as the manner of funding, i.e. the financing costs, vary from company to company. It can however be used effectively for comparing the performance of a company over several years.

Net Profit Margin

Net profit margin shows the after-tax rate a company earns on sales. It indicates the rate on sales that is available for appropriation after all expenses and commitments have been met. In order to facilitate comparison and to get a true picture, non-recurring income and expense should be excluded in the calculation.

$$\text{Net profit margin} = \frac{\text{Net income excluding non-recurring items after tax}}{\text{Sales}}$$

In Kumar Wheels Ltd. the pre-tax income was Rs. 700 lakh. If tax was Rs. 350 lakh, the pre-tax income would be Rs. 350 lakh. Non-recurring income was Rs. 50 lakh.

The net profit margin therefore was:

$$\frac{350-50}{8000} \times 100 = 3.75\ \%$$

The return after tax to shareholders on sales was 3.75%.

The net profit margin also enables a shareholder to determine the additional earnings available to him on increases in sales.

Summary

Margins, thus, help both in understanding the cost structure of a business and evaluating its performance. It is important to remember that low margins are not always bad nor high margins always good. A company may opt to work on very low margins to achieve volumes. On the other hand, a company earning high margins may face falling demand for its products. Investors must always check into the reasons for variations and the various measures mentioned in this chapter will point out to the investor the possible reasons.

Chapter Ten

Cash Flow

In this age of creative accounting, accounting principles are changed, provisions created or written back, and generally accepted accounting principles liberally interpreted or ignored by companies in order to show profits. Shareholders do not realise this when they look at the published profits in the financial statements of companies. It comes therefore as a surprise when a regular profit making company suddenly downs its shutters and goes into liquidation. This occurs when a company is unable to obtain finance or pay its creditors. History is strewn with such examples and investors must always check:

- How much is the company's cash earnings?
- How is the company being financed?
- How is the company using its finance?

The answers to the above can be determined by preparing a statement of sources and uses of funds. Its importance has been recognized in the United States and in many European countries where it is mandatory for a company to publish with its Annual Report, a summary of changes in financial statements which is, in effect, a cash flow statement.

A statement of sources and uses begins with the profit for the year to which are added the increases in liability accounts (sources) and from which are reduced the increases in asset account (uses). The net result shows whether there has been an excess or deficit of funds and how this was financed.

For example, as shown in Table 10.2 Fundamental and Company Limited (Fundamental) reported a profit before tax of Rs. 108.12 lakh. This included, however, other income of Rs. 247.74 lakh, profit on sale of fixed assets of Rs. 112.88 lakh and an amount of Rs. 38.56 lakh withdrawn from a revaluation reserve. If these are deducted, the profit changes to a loss of Rs. 291.06 lakh.

Table 10.1

Fundamental & Co. Ltd.

Balance Sheet as at 31 March

(Rs. lakh)

	Latest Year	*Previous Year*	*Movement*
Sources			
Share Capital	287.79	282.75	0.04
Reserves	3069.32	3083.37	(14.05)
Loan Funds	5058.14	3130.22	1927.92
	8410.25	6496.34	1913.91
Application			
Net Fixed assets	3434.53	3100.06	334.47
Investments	92.37	65.85	26.52
Net Current assets	4878.90	3264.68	1614.22
Misc. expenditure	4.45	65.75	(61.30)
	8410.25	6496.34	1913.91

The changes in Fundamental's Balance Sheet are summarized in Table 10.1, and its Sources and Uses of Funds (S & U) for the latest year ended 31 March are detailed in Table 10.2. The S & U statement shows that the company had a deficit cash flow in its latest year, and that it had to borrow Rs. 1,927.92 lakh to finance its current assets. As it had made a loss, the company paid its dividend on preference shares not out of current profits but from reserves. Further, as inventories and other current assets increased, the possibility that the company was unable to get rid of its surplus stock cannot be ignored.

Table 10.2

Fundamental & Co. Ltd

Sources and Uses of funds for the Latest Year ended 31 March

	(Rs. lakh)
Sources	
Operating Income (loss)	(139.62)
Add depreciation	160.25
Less Profit on sale of fixed assets	(112.88)
Operating Income (loss)	(92.25)
Other Income	247.74
Increase in liabilities	1485.50
Misc. expenditure written off	61.30
Profit on sale of fixed assets	132.14
	1834.43
Application	
Purchase of Fixed Assets (net)	513.98
Purchase of Investments	26.52
Increase in Inventories	1141.38
Increase in sundry debtors	1350.50
Increase in other current assets	88.99
Increase in loans to subsidiary companies	205.92
Increase in loans to others	138.86
Decrease in provisions	14.08

Contd . . .

Table 10.2 (Contd . . .)

	(Rs. lakh)
Decrease in reserves	79.75
	3559.98
Net increase (deficit)	1725.55
Financed by	
Shares Capital	0.06
Increase in cash and bank balances	(202.43)
Increase in loan funds	1927.92
	1725.55

Table 10.3

Dynamic Iron and Steel Company Ltd.

Balance Sheet as at 31 March

			(Rs. crore)
	Latest Year	*Previous Year*	*Movement*
Source			
Share capital	230.12	229.89	0.23
Reserves	1315.36	1194.22	121.14
Loan funds	2051.30	1183.75	867.55
	3596.78	2607.86	988.92
Application			
Net fixed assets	2878.19	1713.79	1164.40
Investments	248.77	571.86	(323.09)
Current assets (net)	469.82	322.21	147.61
	3596.78	2607.86	988.92

The Dynamic Iron and Steel Company Ltd. (DISCO) (*See* Tables 10.3 and 10.4) also had a cash flow deficit although the

Table 10.4

Dynamic Iron and Steel Company Limited

Sources and Uses of funds for the Latest Year ended 31 March

	(Rs. crore)
Sources	
Operating Net Income	278.16
Less payments to employees for prior periods	(13.61)
	264.55
Add: Depreciation	164.89
Funds from Operations	429.44
Sale of Investments	323.09
Decrease in other current assets	0.06
Increase in liabilities	78.34
Increase in provisions	73.20
Total Sources	904.13
Uses	
Net purchases of fixed assets	1329.29
Increase in inventories	221.20
Increase in sundry debtors	24.77
Increase in loans and advances	156.59
Total applications	1731.85
Excess (deficit)	827.72
Financed by	
Issue of shares	1.37
Increases in loans	867.55
Increases in cash and bank balances	(41.20)
	827.72

company made a cash profit of Rs. 429.44 crore. If one assumes this was used to finance the increase in inventories and partially finance assets, the dividend of Rs. 80.55 lakh was once again financed by loans.

Investors must examine a company's cash flow as it reveals exactly where the money came from and how it was utilised. Investors must be concerned if a company is financing either its inventories or paying dividends from borrowings without real growth as that shows a deterioration.

In short, the cash flow or sources and uses of funds statement strips the accounting creativeness from financial statements.

Chapter 11

Conclusion

Fundamental analysis holds that no investment decision should be made without processing and analyzing all relevant information. Its strength lies in the fact that the information analyzed is real as opposed to hunches or assumptions. On the other hand, while fundamental analysis deals with tangible facts, it does tend to ignore the fact that human beings do not always act rationally. Market prices do sometimes deviate from fundamentals. Prices rise or fall due to insider trading, speculation, rumour, and a host of other factors. This was eloquently stated by Gerald Loeb, the author of *The Battle for Investment Survival,* who wrote, "There is no such thing as a final answer to security values. A dozen experts will arrive at 12 different conclusions. It often happens that a few moments later each would alter his verdict if given a chance to reconsider because of a changed condition. Market values are fixed only in part by balance sheets and income statements; much more by hopes and fears of humanity; by greed, ambition, acts of God, invention, financial stress and strain, weather, discovery, fashion and numberless other causes impossible to be listed without omission".

This is true to an extent but the strength of fundamental analysis is that an investment decision is arrived at after analyzing information and making logical assumptions and deductions. And this is where there can be differences in values — the assumptions made by different analysts would differ. Their reasoning will be based on their exposure to the market, their maturity, their knowledge and their gut feel of the market.

Furthermore, fundamental analysis ensures that one does not recklessly buy or sell shares — especially buy. One would buy a share only if its intrinsic value is higher than its book value. This also protects one against possible loss since one would dispose of a share whose market value is higher than its intrinsic value. Hence fundamental analysis supports and encourages safe investing.

No system is fool proof. No system has consistently outperformed the market. There is no system that does not call for human judgement and input. All systems require thought and some assumptions. However, of all the systems that I have experimented with and tried, the one I am most comfortable with is fundamental analysis as it is the most logical and the most meaningful. And this is the system I would urge you to consider as an investor.

Happy investing!

Chapter 12

Fundamental Analysis: Step-by-step

Step-1: Politico-Economic Analysis

1. Politico-economic factors affect an industry and a country.
2. Stable political environment necessary for steady, balanced growth.
3. International events impact industries and companies.
4. Countries need foreign exchange reserves to meet its commitments, pay for imports and service foreign debts.
5. The possibility of the devaluation of one's currency / the appreciation of another currency is a real risk. One can hedge this by entering into forward contracts.
6. Restrictive practices or cartels imposed by countries can affect companies and industries. Investors must determine how sensitive a company is to governmental policies and restrictive policies.
7. Foreign debt can be an enormous burden which would eat into a company's results.
8. Inflation erodes purchasing power. Low inflation indicates stability and companies prosper at such times.

9. Low interest and taxation rates stimulate investment and industry.
10. Domestic savings can accelerate economic growth.
11. Development of a country is dependent on its infrastructure.
12. Budgetary deficits resulting from excess governmental spending stimulate the economy. It also gives rise to increasing demand and increasing inflation.

Economic Cycle

1. Business or economic cycle has direct impact on industry and individual companies. It affects investment decisions, employment, demand and profitability.
2. Four stages of economic cycle are depression, recovery, boom and recession.
3. Investors should determine the stage of the economic cycle before investing. Investors should disinvest just before or during a boom.

Step-2: Industry Analysis

1. Importance of the industry can never be understated. State of industry will affect company performance.
2. It is important to determine cycle. These are entrepreneurial or sunrise, expansion or growth, stabilization or maturity and decline or sunset stages.
3. Investors should purchase in the first two stages and disinvest at the maturity stage.
4. It is better to invest in evergreen industries. Results of cyclical industries are volatile.
5. Investors should consider competition as the greater the competition the lower the profits.
6. It is safer to invest in industries not subject to government controls.

7. Export oriented industries currently favoured by the government.

Step-3: Company Analysis

1. Final stage of fundamental analysis is company analysis.
2. Areas to be examined are the company, the results, ratios and cash flow.

Management

1. Management is the single most important factor to consider in a company. Upon its quality rests the future of the company.
2. In India two main types of management — family and professional.
3. Investors must check on integrity of managers, proven competence, how high is it rated by its peers, how did it perform at times of adversity, the management's depth of knowledge, its innovativeness and professionalism.

The Company

1. It is important to check how company is perceived by its competition and whether it is the market leader in its products or in its segment.
2. The investor must determine the policy a company follows and its plans for growth.
3. Labour relations are important.

The Annual Report

1. The annual report is the primary and most important source of information on a company.
2. The investor must read between and beyond the lines of an annual report to determine the state of the company being considered.

3. The annual report is broken into the directors' report, the auditor's report, the financial statements and the schedules.

The Directors' Report

1. This report gives investors insights into the company.
2. It enunciates the opinion of the directors on the economy, the industry and the political situation.
3. It explains the performance of the company, its plans for diversification, modernization and expansion. It discusses the profits earned and states the dividends proposed.
4. The report, if read properly, can give the investor a good grasp of the workings of the company

The Auditor's Report

1. The auditor represents shareholders and reports to them on the stewardship of the directors and whether the accounts presented do present a true and fair view of the company.
2. Auditors will comment on any changes made in accounting principles and the effect of these changes on the results.
3. Auditors will also comment on any action or method of accounting they do not agree with.
4. Investors must read the auditor's report in detail and in depth as the results can materially change if adjustments are made based on the notes or comments in the auditors report.

Financial Statements

1. Financial statements of a company in an annual report consist of the balance sheet and the profit and loss account. These detail the financial health and performance of the company.
2. The balance sheet details all the assets and liabilities a company has on a particular date. Assets are those that the company owns such as fixed assets (buildings, cars etc.), invest-

ments and current assets (stocks, debtors and cash). Liabilities are those that the company owes (trade creditors, loans, etc.) and the shareholders investment in the company (share capital and reserves).

3. The profit and loss account details numerically the activities the company had undertaken during the accounting period and the result of these activities (profit or loss).
4. Contingent liabilities are also detailed. These are liabilities that may arise on the happening of an event that may never arise (guarantees, bills discounted). The liability crystallizes on the happening of the event.
5. The profit and loss account also details the dividend given (interim) and proposed.

Schedules and Notes to the Accounts

1. Schedules and notes to the accounts are found after the financial statements in an annual report.
2. The schedules detail pertinent information about the items of the balance sheet and profit and loss account.
3. The notes are even more important as they give very important information such as the accounting policies that the company has followed, the contingent liabilities of the companies and the like.
4. It is imperative that the schedules and notes to the accounts be read for a clearer understanding of the company's financial condition.

Ratios

1 No investment should be made without analyzing the financial statements of a company and comparing the company's results with that of earlier years.

2. Ratios express mathematically the relationship between performance figures and/or assets/liabilities in a form that can be easily understood and interpreted.
3. No single ratio tells the complete story.
4. Ratios can be broken into 4 broad categories:

   (a) Profit and Loss Ratios
   (b) Balance Sheet Ratios
   (c) Balance Sheet and Profit and Loss Ratios, and
   (d) Financial Statements to Market Ratios.

5. Ratios may also be grouped into categories that will enable investors to easily determine the company's strengths and weaknesses.

   - Market value ratios reflect the market regard for a share and the period it would take an investor to recover his investment. The common indicators are the price/ earnings ratio and the market to book ratio.
   - Earnings ratios are used to determine the fair market value of shares and to value investments. The ratios calculated are earnings per share, cash earnings per share, dividend per share and dividend payout ratio
   - Profitability is of prime importance and these ratios, return on total assets, return on equity, pre-interest return on assets, pre-interest after tax return on assets and return on total invested capital, assist an investor in determining how well a company is doing *vis a-vis* other companies within the same industry and with reference to its own performance in previous years.
   - Liquidity ratios determine how liquid the company's assets are and whether it can easily meet its obligations. The ratios calculated are the current ratio, the quick or asset test, net current assets, defensive interval and current liability coverage.

- Leverage ratios indicate the extent a company is dependent on borrowings in the form of debentures, short/long term loans and bank overdrafts. The ratios calculated to determine leverage are liabilities to assets ratio, debt to assets ratio, debt to net worth ratio, liabilities to net worth and incremental gearing.
- Debt service capacity ratios indicate whether a company can service its debts. The ones commonly computed are debt coverage, liability coverage, interest cover, fixed charge cover and cash flow surplus.
- Asset management ratios are used to determine how efficiently a company is managing its assets. The more important determinants are the stock utilization ratios, the average collection period, the average payment period, net working investments ratio, total asset utilization and fixed asset utilization.
- Margins indicate the earnings a company makes on its sales. The margins calculated are the gross margin, operating margin, breakeven margin, pre-financing margin, pretax margin and the net profit margin.

Cash Flow

1. Cash flow statements will enable an investor to determine how is the company's cash earnings, how the company is being financed and how it uses the finance received.
2. The statement begins with the cash in hand at the beginning of the period. It then details the sources and amounts of funds received and the manner they were applied ending with the final cash in hand.
3. Its main use is that it strips the accounting statements of creative accounting.

Appendix

Fundamental Analysis: Quick Check List

1. Check the political situation. Is it safe? Are there problems? Could the government be overthrown and could there be difficulties as a consequence?

2. What is revealed by the economic indicators? Is the growth rate reasonable? Have exports improved? How comfortable is the balance of payments position?

3. Check the industry or industries in which the company operates. At what stage of the cycle is the company in? What is its competition? How easy is it to enter or exit the business?

4. Then check the company. The factors one should look at is its management and its annual report. The ratios should be analyzed and the cash flow checked.

5. Finally, before purchasing or selling a share, check its intrinsic value. A decision should only be taken after this is done.

Index